Reclaiming the Lost Art of

Biblical Meditation

Find True Peace in Jesus

ROBERT J. MORGAN

THOMAS NELSON
Since 1798

Published in Nashville, Tennessee, by Thomas Nelson. Thomas Nelson is a registered trademark of HarperCollins Christian Publishing, Inc.

Published in association with Yates & Yates, www.yates2.com.

Thomas Nelson titles may be purchased in bulk for educational, business, fund-raising, or sales promotional use. For information, please e-mail SpecialMarkets@ThomasNelson.com.

ISBN: 978-0-7180-8337-3

Printed in China

17 18 19 20 21 DSC 7 6 5 4 3 2

To Jordan

CONTENTS

Meditation is a lost art today, and Christian people suffer grievously from their ignorance of the practice.

Meditation is the activity of calling to mind, and thinking over, and dwelling on, and applying to oneself, the various things that one knows about the works and ways and purposes and promises of God. It is an activity of holy thought, consciously performed in the presence of God, under the eye of God, by the help of God, as a means of communion with God.[1]

—J. I. PACKER IN *Knowing God*

INTRODUCTION

My eyes stay open through the watches of the night,
that I may meditate on your promises.

—Psalm 119:148

*M*editation is not *new*, and it is not *new age*. God, not the gurus, devised it, and it's based on the Bible, not on Buddha. Biblical meditation is an antidote to the unprecedented stress of our age. In a world where everyone is overwhelmed and undervalued, our survival, sanity, and saintliness depend on reclaiming the lost art of biblical meditation. This habit can dramatically lessen your anxiety in life, reduce your stress, bring new success to your days, and leave you with ocean depths of inner peace.

There are many references to meditation, pondering, and thinking in the Bible, encouraging us to engage our thoughts with His Word. In fact, the words *meditate* and *meditation* occur 21 times in the Bible; the words *think*, *thinking*, and *thoughts*, 252 times. *Mind* is mentioned 163 times, and the word *ponder* is found 9 times.[1] God's approach to *mindfulness* is to have a *mind full* of His Word. That's why the Bible says:

- "Let the word of Christ dwell in you richly" (Colossians 3:16 NKJV).
- "Let this mind be in you which was also in Christ Jesus" (Philippians 2:5 NKJV).
- "Let the words of my mouth and the meditation of my heart be acceptable in Your sight" (Psalm 19:14 NKJV).

If you're a bit allergic to meditation, well . . . get over it. Bible lovers needn't apologize for advocating meditation, for some of the greatest heroes of the faith modeled it for us:

- In the age of the patriarchs, Isaac went out at dusk to meditate in the fields (Genesis 24:63).
- The Lord told Joshua about the Law of God: "Meditate on it day and night. . . . Then you will be prosperous and successful" (Joshua 1:8).
- The Psalmist pictured those who meditate day and night as fruitful trees by rivers of water (Psalm 1:2–3).
- Jeremiah said, "When your words came, I ate them; they were my joy and my heart's delight" (Jeremiah 15:16).
- The Virgin Mary treasured God's words and pondered them in her heart (Luke 2:19).
- Jesus advised His followers to "hear the word, accept it, meditate on it, act on it, and bear fruit" (Mark 4:20 THE VOICE).

- The apostle Paul told us to think about things that are true, noble, and gracious, and to meditate on those things (Philippians 4:8, see THE MESSAGE).
- The writer of Hebrews told us to "fix [our] thoughts on Jesus" (Hebrews 3:1).

Meditation is a habit recommended in the Bible; yet, whenever I bring up the subject, some people look at me as if I'd suggested they jaywalk across a busy street. There's a reason for the confusion. Modern meditation, as it is commonly viewed, is not biblical meditation. In recent years, New Agers have hijacked the habit, and I was actually there when it happened. One day, in 1970, as I walked across the quadrangle of the college I attended in Bristol, Tennessee, I heard exciting news. Maharishi Mahesh Yogi was coming—or maybe he was sending someone—to teach us Transcendental Meditation (TM). When the day came, we packed the room for the mysterious robed man, and he taught us a few rudimentary TM techniques. He told us to sit properly, breathe deeply, and empty our minds. While interesting, the swami lost me somewhere between karma and mantra, and I didn't fall into Zen.

The next year I transferred to another school, Columbia International University, where I met a group of people—the Navigators—who also extolled the value of meditation, but they viewed it differently, as a biblical habit. They believed we should constantly memorize, visualize, and personalize God's Word. The Navigators illustrate this point using the image of the human hand: First, getting a grip on God's Word requires the four fingers of hearing it, reading it, studying it, and memorizing it. But the thumb that strengthens the grip is meditation.

Once we have a grip on the Bible, our feet go into action, putting into practice what we're learning.

Biblical meditation is the habit that allows us to pause long enough to be still and to know that God is God. It leads us to spiritual growth, emotional strength, deepening intimacy with the Lord, and soul-steadying peace.

There is healing and holy power in pondering, picturing, and personalizing passages of Scripture from God's Word. And that's my simple definition for true meditation:

> *Biblical meditation is the powerful practice*
> *of pondering, personalizing, and practicing Scripture.*

It really is as simple as that. While there's value in breathing exercises and relaxation techniques (I'll touch on those later), biblical meditation is more than contemplating the sensation of air passing through our noses and into our lungs. It doesn't involve draining our heads of content, but rather filling them with the specific Bible verses and passages God brings to our minds at certain times. That's part of the ministry of the Holy Spirit, whose job it is to remind us of everything Jesus has said to us (John 14:26).

Biblical meditation is not just *reading* Scripture or *studying* Scripture or even thinking *about* Scripture; instead, it is *thinking* Scripture—contemplating, visualizing, and personifying the precious truths God has given us. Like water flowing through a fountain or oil through a machine, Scripture should be constantly circulating through our minds so that we become God-conditioned. In the process, we start to look at things as He does, which is the essence of wisdom—seeing life from His point of view. Our attitudes become healthier, and our emotions fall into line.[2]

Biblical meditation is an easy habit to begin. It's as portable as your brain, as available as your imagination, as near as your Bible—and the benefits are immediate. I've written this little book to give you some of the whys and hows of meditation, and to show you how it will draw you closer to the Lord and give you fresh insights into His ways, His will, and His Word.

> Like water flowing through a fountain or oil through a machine, Scripture should be constantly circulating through our minds.

Meditate on these things; give yourself entirely to them,
that your progress may be evident to all.

—1 TIMOTHY 4:15 NKJV

WHY IS BIBLICAL
MEDITATION IMPORTANT?

> I call to remembrance my song in the night;
> I meditate within my heart,
> And my spirit makes diligent search.
>
> —Psalm 77:6 NKJV

*H*arriet Tubman was a spy who, even in moments of extreme danger, demonstrated nothing but raw, calm courage. Born into slavery in the 1820s, Harriet was nearly killed when her master hurled a metal object at her. She staged a daring escape in 1849, then spent years rescuing hundreds out of slavery and leading them to safety. Her code name was Moses, because she never lost a single escapee. During the Civil War, she became a secret agent for the Union Army, working behind enemy lines to scout out the territory. Despite a bounty on her head, she always managed to evade capture.

A devout follower of Christ, Tubman spent much time learning, memorizing, and meditating on various verses in the Bible, such as her beloved Isaiah 16:3: "Hide the fugitives, do not betray the refugees." As she pondered the passages, she turned them into prayers, and in prayer she learned to practice God's presence.

"I prayed all the time," she told her biographer, "about my work, everywhere; I was always talking to the Lord. When I went to the horse trough to wash my face and took up the water in my hands, I said, 'Oh, Lord, wash me, make me clean.' When I took up the towel to wipe my face and hands, I cried, 'Oh, Lord, for Jesus' sake, wipe away all my sins!' When I took up the broom and began to sweep, I groaned, 'Oh, Lord, whatsoever sin there be in my heart, sweep it out, Lord, clear and clean.'"[1]

In this way, Harriet forged a personality of action and audacity. She built a mind-set that transcended her background and transformed her life. And we can do the same. As we habitually hide God's Word in our hearts, claim those special verses that seem to have our names on them, ponder and picture them, and turn them into unceasing praise and prayer, we will practice the presence of God—and He will transform us into agents of audacious boldness for His glory.

Let's start with the basics. According to Romans 12:2, we

Quick Tip: Use sticky notes to post key verses at your bedside, on the bathroom mirror, on the dashboard of your car, and other places where you'll have opportunities to ponder them.

are transformed by the renewing of our minds as God changes the way we think. That verse is part of a chain of thoughts in Romans that provides a biblical basis for understanding the power of meditation. These verses explain what's wrong with our minds, why we struggle with our thoughts, and how we can bring health and healing to our brainwaves and inner selves.

Without Christ, Our Minds Are Dark Places

Imagine a university where the library is open only on moonless nights and all lights are prohibited. The students have access to all the books, desks, and study carrels, but they must pursue their studies in total blackness. Expensive volumes fill the reading rooms—some of them rare and valuable. Students are free to move among the bookshelves and remove any resources they want. But everything is done in darkness—no lamps, no candles, no flashlights, no light of any kind. Total blackout.

That's a pretty accurate picture of a world trying to learn, trying to think, and trying to meditate without the light of the life of Christ.

Referring to fallen humanity, Paul wrote:

> Their *thinking became futile* and their *foolish hearts were darkened.* . . . They exchanged the truth about God for a lie. . . . Furthermore, just as

they *did not think it worthwhile to retain the knowledge of God,* so God gave them over to *a depraved mind.* . . . They have *no understanding.* (Romans 1:21, 25, 28, 31, emphasis mine)

Without Christ, our thoughts are as dark as midnight. Apart from God's grace in Christ, our minds are corrupt (Titus 1:15), depraved (2 Timothy 3:8), anxious (Deuteronomy 28:65), cunning (Psalm 64:6), closed (Isaiah 44:18), warped (Proverbs 12:8), "puffed up with idle notions" (Colossians 2:18), and "always learning but never able to come to a knowledge of the truth" (2 Timothy 3:7). As God said in the days of Noah, without Christ, every inclination of the thoughts of the human heart is only evil all the time (Genesis 6:5).

How can that be? The human brain is the greatest marvel of God's creation—more complex than the largest star or the smallest atom. But it was corrupted by Satan's lies. Like a finely tuned engine, our brains are designed for only one fuel—Truth. The Truth that comes from God. The Truth that pervades His creation. The Truth found in His perfect character and infallible Word.

Jesus Turns the Light On

The only way to change your life is to change your mind, and that requires changing the lordship and leadership of your heart.

> The only way to change your life is to change your mind, and that requires changing the lordship and leadership of your heart.

When Christ becomes your Savior and Lord, He turns the light on inside you.

That's because Jesus came as the light of the world. Romans 3:22–25 says:

> This righteousness is given through faith in Jesus Christ to all who believe. . . . for all have sinned and fall short of the glory of God, and all are justified freely by His grace through the redemption that came by Christ Jesus. God presented Christ as a sacrifice of atonement, through the shedding of His blood—to be received by faith.

Romans 5:1–2 summarizes it this way:

> Therefore, since we have been justified through faith, we have peace with God through our Lord Jesus Christ, through whom we have gained access by faith into this grace in which we now stand.

When we come to Jesus, He shines His wisdom into our hearts and inspires our thoughts. He helps us focus on God and gain perspective. As Romans 6:17 says, "But thanks be to God that, though you used to be slaves to sin, you have come to obey from your heart *the pattern of teaching* that has now claimed your allegiance" (emphasis mine).

We Still Struggle with Shadows

Yet, even after receiving Christ as our Savior, we still struggle with our thoughts. Dark shadows dance on the walls of our minds. We are conflicted. Paul himself admitted in Romans 7:23 that his sinful nature waged war *"against the law of my mind . . . making me a prisoner of the law of sin at work within me"* (emphasis mine).

We can easily relate to Paul's confession, for this is the universal testimony of every believer. We may be followers of Christ for many years, but we still struggle with thoughts that are anxious, covetous, lustful, angry, resentful, fearful, or depressed.

The process of spiritual growth involves increasing the wattage of the light that shines in our hearts and minds—and that light comes only from our Lord:

> For God, who said, "Let light shine out of darkness," made His
> light shine in our hearts to give us the light of the knowledge of
> God's glory displayed in the face of Christ. (2 Corinthians 4:6)

Let the Holy Spirit Govern Our Minds

To help with this wattage increase, we have a Master Electrician—the Holy Spirit. He understands the wiring of our minds. He knows when the lines are overloaded and when we are about to blow a fuse—or already have! He understands when our energy runs low, our emotions short-circuit, or the bulbs just simply burn out. He is able to switch currents from negative to positive.

It's all described in Romans 8, one of the most power-packed chapters in the Bible. Here we learn how the Holy Spirit takes the redemption of Christ and uses it to rewire our hearts with biblical truth. The Spirit grounds us in the Word. He is the great Transformer.

Romans 8:5–6 says:

> Those who live according the flesh have their *minds set* on what the flesh desires; but those who live in accordance with the Spirit have their *minds set* on what the Spirit desires. The *mind governed by the flesh* is death, but the *mind governed by the Spirit* is life and peace. (emphasis mine)

Jesus of Nazareth died and rose again to illuminate our minds with His light; and as the Spirit governs our thought lives we experience both life and light. This is resurrection thinking. This is biblical thinking, and this is where meditation comes in.

We Are Transformed Daily as God Renews Our Minds

Do you want to have greater resistance to temptation, more wisdom in decision making, and increased influence among your friends? Each of these skills is rooted in your mental patterns and in meditation.

We must remember that rewiring our minds is an ongoing spiritual operation. Though we are redeemed at Calvary, the process of repairing the mind isn't a onetime event. It's a process, which is explained in Romans 12:

> Therefore, I urge you, brothers and sisters, in view of God's mercy,
> to offer your bodies as a living sacrifice . . . Do not conform to the
> pattern of this world, but be transformed by *the renewing of your mind.*
> Then you will be able to test and approve what God's will is—his
> good, pleasing and perfect will. (verses 1–2, emphasis mine)

To fulfill God's good plan and accomplish His will, we must stop thinking the way the world thinks and start thinking the way He does.

How? With biblical meditation. It's our greatest tool and most effective technique.

As we ponder, picture, and personalize God's Word, we

begin looking at life through His lens, viewing the world from His perspective. Our thoughts become happier and holier and brighter—and so do we.

We practice biblical meditation by noting, quoting, and devoting ourselves to whatever passage of Scripture we're reading or studying, based on the premise that God's Word is flawless, faultless, and unfailing. Meditation helps and heals the mind while shoring up the soul. It lessens anxiety, reduces stress, and generates peace.

It's springtime as I'm writing this, and last night my wife, Katrina, and I had supper on our back porch. The birds were fluttering around the bird feeders, and the geraniums were blooming in the pots. We talked about meditation, and Katrina recalled that Isaac was the first person in the Bible who is specifically said to have meditated. Genesis 24:63 says, "He [Isaac] went out to the field one evening to meditate."

"I wonder what he meditated about," Katrina said. "The Bible hadn't yet been written, so he didn't have much tangible Scripture. But he was surrounded by the beauty of God's creation, he had a godly heritage, and his spiritual experiences in life had been rich. He was the miracle son of Abraham and Sarah, born in fulfillment of divine promises. As a youth, he'd experienced the sacrifice of Mount Moriah, and he had heard the voice of an angel. He knew God's promise for his descendants, though he still had no wife and was grieving over the death of his mother.

Quick Tip: Include biblical meditation in your vacation planning. Think ahead of a passage you want to ponder while walking on the beach, sitting on the balcony, or resting in the hammock.

"I suppose he simply reviewed his life," continued Katrina, "composed his heart, thought about God, listened to the birds and brooks, prayed some, and wondered by faith what God was going to do with him."

Interestingly, Isaac's meditation was interrupted by the arrival of a caravan returning from Mesopotamia and bearing the woman who would soon become his wife.

As we meditate, God guides and changes our thoughts, helps us process our griefs and sorrows, enables us to soak up the wonder of His greatness, and prepares us for what He has planned for us. That's what He did for the heroes of Scripture, and that's what He'll do for us.

As we end this chapter, why not turn this old hymn into a personal prayer?

> *May the mind of Christ, my Savior,*
> *Live in me from day to day,*
> *By His love and power controlling*
> *All I do and say.*[2]

For a free downloadable group study guide for this book as well as free personal audio meditation guides, visit www.robertjmorgan.com/meditation.

BIBLICAL MEDITATION:

Focusing on the Wonder of God and Gaining Perspective

I remember the days of old;
I meditate on all Your works;
I muse on the work of Your hands.

—Psalm 143:5 NKJV

*I*n her book *Lessons I Learned in the Dark,* Jennifer Rothschild describes her fear of flying after the catastrophic events of September 11, 2001. Threats to airlines were a daily reality, she said, yet she was scheduled to fly every weekend that fall. She was fearful, and the atmosphere in airports and planes was tense. "I remember getting on my knees before God and telling Him that

I was fearful," she wrote. "Immediately, this verse came to my mind: 'When I am afraid, I will trust in you' (Psalm 56:3)."

Jennifer began claiming and contemplating that verse. "God knows that sometimes fear and trust share the same heartbeat," she said. "As I meditated on the verse, I suddenly realized that *I am afraid* describes a condition and that *I will trust* describes a volition. The verse is definitive: My volition can change my condition."[1]

By meditating on Psalm 56:3, Jennifer found the courage and peace she needed for every trip. She discovered the secret of replacing the lower thoughts of fear with the higher thoughts of faith.

Here, then, is another definition of biblical meditation: it's the act of claiming and contemplating specific passages God gives us during life's events. In meditation, God's thoughts lift our hearts to a heavenly level. It's how we shift our focus from the lowlands of our problems to the highlands of His perspective.

Three passages in the Bible talk about exchanging our "lower" thoughts for God's "higher" ones—Isaiah 55, Colossians 3, and James 3.

God's Thoughts Are Not Our Thoughts

In Isaiah 55:8 the Lord tells us, "My thoughts are not your thoughts, neither are your ways my ways."

Quick Tip: Learn to meditate with pad and pencil. Print out a passage and mark up the page, underlining, dissecting, listing, and analyzing. Remember meditation isn't a passive activity. It's a way of engaging your attention on a particular scripture.

In other words, God does not think as we do. He views things from an eternal angle. The Creator of the human brain enjoys an infinite mind that instantly grasps every detail of everything in every way, in every place, from every side, at every time—whether past, present, or future. God cannot learn anything new, and He can never misunderstand. Nothing in heaven escapes His notice, nor is anything on earth beyond His knowledge. His mind is never overwhelmed by the largest mystery, and it never overlooks the tiniest molecule.

> Nothing in heaven escapes His notice, nor is anything on earth beyond His knowledge.

God knows the temperature of every star, the composition of every planet, the size of every galaxy, and the course of every comet. He knows the shape of each snowflake and the design of every seashell. He understands the mysteries of the depths below and the heights above. He knows what lies beyond the galaxies and beyond the grave. His wisdom is as high as the heavens, as deep as the oceans, as broad as the cosmos, and as long as eternity. And His thoughts are not our thoughts.

God has instant access to every fact of reality and to every factor of every decision. His intelligence is limitless, His brilliance boundless, His perception unfailing and unerring. He neither panics nor puzzles over the problems of His creation, for His thoughts are not our thoughts.

His plans are foolproof. His reflections are reviving. His intuition is unerring. The Lord will never forget or forsake you. In His omniscience, it is simply impossible. He knows all about you—every ancestor in your family tree, every strand in your DNA, every quirk in your personality, every bump and bruise in your childhood, and every trial, tragedy, hurt, and heartache you've ever encountered or ever will. He numbers both your steps and the very hairs of your head. He sees every rejection and failure. He rejoices in every victory and records all your faithful deeds.

According to Psalm 139, our God searches us and knows us. He sees when we sit and when we rise; He perceives our thoughts from afar. He discerns our going out and our lying down and is familiar with all our ways. How precious are all His thoughts (Psalm 139:1–3, 17)!

God's thoughts are higher than ours, but He has sent His thoughts down to us in ink drops that fall from heaven like raindrops in a drought. Isaiah 55 continues:

> "As the rain and the snow come down from heaven and do not return to it without watering the earth and making it bud and

flourish, so that it yields seed for the sower and bread for the eater, so is my word that goes out from my mouth. It will not return to me empty, but will accomplish what I desire and achieve the purpose for which I sent it." (verses 10–11)

God has sent His thoughts down to us in an infallible, understandable, incredible Book. And by meditating on His thoughts as encoded in the Bible, our lives will be watered with His Word. His thoughts will seep in like rainwater soaking a garden; they are designed to nurture and produce a crop of heavenly blessings. Verse 12 says: "You will go out in joy and be led forth in peace; the mountains and hills will burst into song before you, and all the trees of the field will clap their hands."

But that's not all! As we meditate on His thoughts, the barren places of our lives begin to flourish. Verse 13 continues, "Instead of the thornbush will grow the juniper, and instead of briers the myrtle will grow. This will be for the LORD's renown, for an everlasting sign, that will endure forever."

Though we will never fully understand the thoughts of God, meditaion allows us to thrive by aligning our thoughts more closely with His. The Lord is patient, because He knows the outcome. He is cheerful, for He has a plan. He is all-powerful, so He isn't afraid. And as we contemplate Him through His Word, we grow in our own patience, cheerfulness, and courage.

Quick Tip: The best meditation doesn't just occur with miscellaneous random verses. It comes from a systematic study of the Word of God. You might try my habit of reading today where I left off yesterday. Right now I'm reading through Exodus, pondering the book one verse and chapter at a time, day after day. Meditation can be spontaneous, but it can also be methodical. As we meditate on His thoughts, the barren places of our lives begin to flourish.

Meditation is the process by which our thoughts come to mirror God's thoughts, letting us see things in His terms, from His perspective, and with His wisdom.

Set Our Minds on Things Above

Solomon Ginsburg was a man who knew the power of giving himself to the meditation of Scripture. He was a Messianic Jew who lived a hundred years ago and traveled the world preaching the gospel. In 1911, he decided to head to America. His route took him to Lisbon, where he planned to cross the Bay of Biscay to London, and from there to travel on to the States.

> Meditation is the process by which our thoughts come to mirror God's thoughts.

Like Jennifer Rothschild, Ginsburg was apprehensive about his travels. Arriving in Lisbon, he found the bulletin boards plastered with weather telegrams warning of terrific storms raging on the Bay of Biscay. It was dangerous sailing, and he was advised to delay his trip a week. His ticket allowed him to do that, and he prayed about it, mulling over a verse he had read that day—Deuteronomy 2:7: "The LORD your God has blessed you in all the work of your hands. He has watched over your journey."

The Lord seemed to assure Ginsburg his worldwide travels were under divine protection. Ginsburg boarded ship at once, crossed without incident, and caught the *Majestic* in London. His transatlantic voyage was smooth and restful. Only after arriving in the United States did Solomon learn that had he delayed his trip in Lisbon, he would have arrived in London just in time to have boarded the *Titanic*.[2]

Somehow—and I don't know how it is—the Lord whispers words of wisdom and guidance into our ears as we meditate on Scripture. He keeps us from the shipwrecks of life as we let His word dwell in us richly. He enables us to set our minds on things above, not on earthly things.

Perhaps the apostle Paul meditated on Isaiah 55 before writing these words in Colossians 3:

> Since, then, you have been raised with Christ, *set your hearts on things above*, where Christ is, seated at the right hand of God. *Set your minds on things above*, not on earthly things. For you died, and your life is now hidden with Christ in God. (verses 1–3, emphasis mine)

How do we set our hearts and minds on things above? Verse 16 gives the answer: "Let the word of Christ dwell in you richly in all wisdom" (NKJV).

In his sermon on Colossians 3:16, Charles Spurgeon explained:

In order that [the Word of Christ] may dwell in you, it must first enter into you. You must really know the spiritual meaning of it. You must believe it, live upon it, drink it in—you must let it soak into your innermost being as the dew saturated the fleece of Gideon. It is not enough to have the Bible on the shelf—it is infinitely better to have its Truths stored up within your soul. . . . There is no book so fitted or so suited to us as the Bible. There is no book that knows us so well. There is no book that is so much at home with us. There is no book that has so much power over us if we will but give ourselves up to it![3]

Gain the Wisdom from Above

One other passage in Scripture uses language quite similar to Isaiah 55 and Colossians 3. It's James 3:14–17, which says:

> If you harbor bitter envy and selfish ambition in your hearts, do not boast about it or deny the truth. Such "wisdom" does not come down from heaven but is earthly, unspiritual, demonic. For where you have envy and selfish ambition, there you find disorder and every evil practice.
>
> But the wisdom that comes from heaven is first of all pure; then peace-loving, considerate, submissive, full of mercy and good fruit, impartial and sincere.

There is wisdom from below and there is wisdom from above—an earthly perspective and a heavenly perspective, our thoughts and God's thoughts. Without the light of Scripture, our world and its thinkers live in the lowlands, in the mental dungeons and basements of reality. Our society operates on the lowest levels, just as in the days of Noah when "the LORD saw how great the wickedness of the human race had become on the earth, and that every inclination of the thoughts of the human heart was only evil all the time" (Genesis 6:5).

James described this sort of thinking as wisdom *from below*. The wisdom *from above*, however, is the opposite—pure, peaceful, considerate, submissive, full of mercy, fruitful, unprejudiced, and sincere.

But how do we shift from our lower thoughts to God's higher ones? According to an earlier passage in James, it's by having the Word of God planted in us, looking intently into it, and not forgetting what it says, but doing it. James 1:21–25 says,

> Humbly accept the word planted in you, which can save you. Do not merely listen to the word . . . Do what it says. . . . Whoever *looks intently* into the perfect law that gives freedom, and *continues* in it . . . they will be blessed in what they do. (emphasis mine)

The Greek word for "looking intently" is used of Peter in

Quick Tip: If you're meditating on a verse, try sharing it with someone during the day. If you want to be a little radical about it, see what happens when you determine to share your verse with the first person you meet during the course of the day. You might just find that your meditation is turning into a witness for Christ.

Luke 24:12 as he gazed wonderingly into the vacated tomb of Christ. As we gaze into the Scripture and ponder what it says, not forgetting it but putting it into practice, we'll increasingly think as God does. We'll be lifted from the negative thinking of the world around us, and we'll begin to understand things from a higher perspective.

"Foolish people meditate upon foolish things," said Susannah Henderson, a Bible teacher of yesteryear. "Wise people meditate upon wise things."[4]

By meditation, we view our circumstances differently. We see our world from another angle. And because His thoughts are becoming our thoughts as we develop the mind of Christ, we are then able to relax, to trust, to quiet ourselves, and to discover peace and confidence.

This happens in the simplest ways at the most ordinary times. I'm writing these words in California, where I had a weekend of speaking engagements. With the time change and schedule disruptions, I didn't sleep well, waking in the wee hours and troubled by all those vague worries that nibble away at the corners of our minds in the darkness. Among other things, I happened to remember that California has earthquakes. I was on the sixth floor of a large hotel, and I wondered if my clothes were nearby and if I could remember the escape route. A silly fear coiled around my mind.

I've conditioned myself to meditate at such moments. Half-asleep and half-awake, I started quoting Psalm 46: "God is our refuge and strength, a very present help in trouble. Therefore we will not fear, even though the earth be removed, and though the mountains be carried into the midst of the sea" (verses 1–2, NKJV). The words came almost subconsciously, but they soothed my mind and allowed me to relax so I could fall asleep again.

We need the thoughts of God—the perspective of eternity, the wisdom from above, and the mind of Christ. As we meditate on Scripture deliberately and daily, our wisdom is enriched, and we can say along with the prophet Habakkuk: "The Sovereign LORD is my strength; he makes my feet like the feet of a deer, he enables me to tread on the heights" (3:19).

With meditation you can focus on the wonder of God, gain a higher perspective, and tap into His wisdom from above. These things, then, become not only your shield in a world embroiled in a spiritual war; they also become your weapons. For . . .

[t]he weapons we fight with are not the weapons of the world. On the contrary, they have the divine power to demolish strongholds. We demolish arguments and every pretension that sets itself up against the knowledge of

God, and we take captive every thought to make it obedient to Christ.

2 Corinthians 10:4–5

For a free downloadable group study guide for this book as well as free personal audio meditation guides, visit www.robertjmorgan.com/meditation.

3

BIBLICAL MEDITATION:

Seeing Yourself as the Lord Sees You

Meditate on these things; give yourself entirely to
them, that your progress may be evident to all.

—1 TIMOTHY 4:15

The National Institutes of Health report that 18 million people in the United States have practiced meditation,[1] which is 8 percent of the population. Most do it because, as thousands of studies have shown, meditation builds us up and calms us down. Other studies indicate meditation makes our minds stronger and faster, just as exercise does for the body.

None of this is exactly new. Long ago, King Solomon said, "For as he thinketh in his heart, so is he" (Proverbs 23:7 KJV).

29

Quick Tip: Take a Bible walk.
Jot down a verse or passage
of Scripture, go walking for
exercise, and think about what
that verse says, what it means,
and what it means to you.
Think about how you'd teach
or preach this verse to others if
given the opportunity.

It's not surprising that positive thinking and meditation yield some benefits. Thus, it should be even less surprising to note the benefits of *biblical meditation* to those who let the Word of God dwell in them richly. Imagine our minds filled with the very thoughts of God—enriched with His wisdom, coached with His counsel, nourished with His commands, drenched in His truth, trusting in His promises. Biblical meditation builds us up and allows us to see ourselves and our lives as the Lord sees us. Let's examine these truths through the lens of two fathomless passages about this—Isaiah 26:3–4 and 2 Peter 1:3–4.

Be Nourished . . . by Thinking About the Person of God

In 2003, my friends Bert and Dianne Tippett traveled to North Carolina to be present for their son Brian's painful bone marrow test. That night in bed, Bert and Dianne throbbed with inner pain, terribly worried about Brian's cancer. Bert was angry, and Dianne was crying. But as they began praying together, an overwhelming peace entered the room and settled on them, and they both fell asleep. The grip of fear and anxiety was broken.

Five years later, Bert himself was diagnosed with cancer, but the peace of God never left him. When people asked how he was doing, he said, "I'm enjoying perfect peace," a secret he learned by meditating on Isaiah 26:3–4:

> You will keep him in perfect peace, whose mind is stayed on You, because he trusts in You. Trust in the Lord forever, for in Yah, the Lord, is everlasting strength. (NKJV)

Look at the two phrases at the front and back of the passage: "perfect peace" and "everlasting strength." That's the condition of the person whose mind is stayed on the Lord and whose heart trusts Him forever. The phrase "perfect peace" is actually "shalom, shalom." The Hebrews didn't have a term for superlative peace, so they simply took their great word "shalom" and doubled it. The message for us is that the Lord wants to double our peace and our calmness. He wants to impart strength for our days.

> The Lord wants to double our peace and our calmness. He wants to impart strength for our days.

Heavenly peace comes through meditation and trust. We must "stay" our minds on Him and trust in Yah—Yahweh, Jehovah, the Lord—forever.

What does it mean to "stay" our minds on the Lord? It means to keep our minds focused on Him, to think about Him, to be devoted to Him, and to be conscious of His person, His presence, and His providence over our lives. Jesus told us to love the Lord our God with all our minds (Matthew 22:37), and the Psalmist said, "Blessed are those who fear the LORD, who find great delight in his commands" (Psalm 112:1).

Meditation is *staying* our minds on the Lord, loving Him with every thought, fearing Him, and delighting in His commands.

When Harry Truman became president, he worried about losing touch with common, everyday Americans, so he would often go out and be among them. Those were in simpler days, when the president could take a walk like everyone else. One evening, Truman decided to take a walk down to the Memorial Bridge on the Potomac River. When he grew curious about the mechanism that raised and lowered the bridge, he made his way across the catwalks and came upon the bridge tender, who was eating his evening supper out of a tin bucket.

The man showed absolutely no surprise when he looked up and saw the best-known and most powerful man in the world. He just swallowed his food, wiped his mouth, smiled, and said, "You know, Mr. President, I was just thinking of you."

According to Truman's biographer, David McCullough, it was a greeting that Truman adored and never forgot.[2]

The Lord adores it when He finds us just thinking about Him. Remember Fanny Crosby's old hymn, "Redeemed, How I Love to Proclaim It"?

Quick Tip: Write your own devotional book. Take a verse every day, meditate on it, and write a paragraph about its meaning to you. Consider posting your meditation, when appropriate, on social media.

I think of my blessed Redeemer,
I think of Him all the day long:
I sing, for I cannot be silent;
His love is the theme of my song.[3]

When we meet the Lord daily, when we open His Word, when we whisper a prayer, when we walk with Him, we're staying our minds on Him and fixing our thoughts on Jesus. That leads to trusting Him more and experiencing more of the fathomless *shalom, shalom* of Him who said, "Peace I leave with you; my peace I give you. I do not give to you as the world gives. Do not let your hearts be troubled and do not be afraid" (John 14:27).

Be Strengthened . . . by Claiming the Promises of God

The second passage is from the pen of Simon Peter, who wrote these words:

> His divine power has given us everything we need for a godly life through our knowledge of him who called us by his own glory and goodness. Through these he has given us his very great and precious promises, so that through them you may participate in the divine nature. (2 Peter 1:3–4)

Pay attention to the progression of thought here:

- God's divine power gives us everything we need.
- What we most need is a godly life.
- A godly life comes from our knowledge of Him who called us by His glory and goodness.
- Through His glory and goodness, He has given us His promises.
- His promises are very great and precious.
- Through His promises, we can claim that godly life and participate in the divine nature.

High on a bookshelf in my office is a tattered little book written in 1848 that helped me better understand the significance of this. The title page says, *"A Collection of the Sweet Assuring Promises of Scripture, or The Believers Inheritance,* by Samuel Clarke, D.D."

Clarke loved young people and taught a weekly Bible class for students. He wanted them to discover the power of God's promises for their lives, so he compiled a little book of biblical promises for them to memorize and on which to meditate. In his introduction Clarke wrote:

> A fixed, constant attention to the promises, and a firm belief in them, would prevent solicitude and anxiety about the concerns

of this life. It would keep the mind quiet and composed in every change, and support and keep up our sinking spirits under the several troubles of life.

Christians deprive themselves of their most solid comforts by their unbelief and forgetfulness of God's promises. For there is no extremity so great, but there are promises suitable to it, and abundantly sufficient for our relief in it.

A thorough acquaintance with the promises would be of the greatest advantage in prayer. . . . And with what fervor of spirit and strength of faith may he enforce his prayers by pleading the several gracious promises which are expressly to his case![4]

In reading the memoirs of missionary Rosalind Goforth of China, I came across an interesting account involving *Clarke's Bible Promises*. Rosalind and her family were trapped in the city of Hsin-tein during the Boxer Rebellion. Multitudes were being slaughtered throughout China, and a bloodthirsty mob gathered around the inn where the Goforths were staying.

Suddenly, without the slightest warning, I was seized with an overwhelming fear of what might be awaiting us. It was not the fear of death, but of probable torture, that took such awful hold of me. I thought, "Can this be the Christian courage I have looked for?" I went by myself and prayed for victory, but no help came.

Just then some one [*sic*] called us to a room for prayer before getting into the carts. Scarcely able to walk for trembling, and utterly ashamed that others should see my state of panic . . . I managed to reach a bench beside which my husband stood. He drew from his pocket a little book, *Clarke's Scripture Promises*, and read the verses his eyes first fell upon. . . . The effect of these words at such a time was remarkable. All realized that God was speaking to us. Never was there a message more directly given to mortal man from his God than that message to us. From almost the first verse my whole soul seemed flooded with a great peace; all trace of panic vanished; and I felt God's presence was with us. Indeed, His presence was so real it could scarcely have been more so had we seen a visible form.[5]

If you don't have a copy of *Clarke's Bible Promises*, don't worry. You don't need one. You have something better—a Bible packed with the very great and precious promises of God, which will give you enough fodder for a lifetime of meditation.

Search out His promises for yourself and meditate on them. Take His promises seriously—more seriously than your problems. As you stay your mind on the Promise Giver, you'll never face a day, or a disappointment, or a disaster without finding a word from God to sustain you.

As we read God's Word each day and deliberately think

about it—focusing our minds on His person and claiming His promises—we're built up, and we come to understand our world and ourselves more clearly.

That's what Henrietta Mears discovered on a train from Minnesota to California. Henrietta was a Hollywood Bible teacher who inspired generations of young people and helped propel Billy Graham and Bill Bright into their global ministries. She led the lost souls of Hollywood, both stars and strays, to the Lord. She built a publishing empire, taught and wrote, traveled and spoke, and served on the staff of Hollywood Presbyterian Church. Hundreds of workers trace their call to ministry to her influence.

According to her biographer, Henrietta's energy came from meditation. In 1934, for example, she boarded a train in Minneapolis for home. In her little compartment, she opened her Bible to Galatians 5 and studied the promises of God regarding the fruits of the Spirit. Stretching out in her Pullman berth, she mulled over the passage. "Do I really have the fruits of the Spirit?" she asked herself. "How much of my joy and peace is dependent upon things and conditions and people around me, and how much comes from the Spirit of God?"

> Take His promises seriously—more seriously than your problems.

Quick Tip: Slowly read a passage or chapter into the voice recorder on your phone, and then play it back as you ride to work or school. Listen to it several times a day. Soon you'll be learning it without strenuous memorization.

Her mind went to another verse she planned to use in her lesson—Romans 6:11: "In the same way, count yourselves dead to sin but alive to God."

The train swayed from side to side as it sped through the darkness, the wheels clacking against the tracks. Lying in her berth, Henrietta mulled over the verses. She connected the Romans passage with the one in Galatians. She prayed over the words. Suddenly a light switched on inside her, and she sat up in bed. "Alive to God!" she said. "That's the secret."

And that *is* the secret. It does no good us to be dead to sin if we're not alive to God; but if we're alive to God, He will produce the fruit.

That night, kneeling by her bed, Henrietta prayed, "Lord, I want to be alive unto You! I want to be alive to You and then I know that the fruits of the Spirit will follow." She saw herself alive to God in a fresh way, and her excitement overflowed. Arriving in California, she gathered her class and said, "I want to share with you a wonderful discovery."[6]

Life is full of wonderful discoveries when we meditate on God's Word. Turn off the television, find a quiet place, and open the Bible. Learn to look for verses that seem written just for you today. Take them into your heart. Stay your mind on Him and dwell on His very great and precious promises. You'll see yourself and your life in divine terms. Soon you'll be saying to others, "I want to share with you a wonderful discovery!"

Hear this, all you peoples;
    listen, all who live in this world,
both low and high,
    rich and poor alike:
My mouth will speak words of wisdom;
    the meditation of my heart will give you understanding.

—Psalm 49:1–3

For a free downloadable group study guide for this book as well as free personal audio meditation guides, visit www.robertjmorgan.com/meditation.

BIBLICAL MEDITATION:

Calming Your Spirit and Finding Peace

May my meditation be sweet to Him;
I will be glad in the Lord.

—PSALM 104:34 NKJV

*B*ut Mary treasured up all these things and pondered them in her heart"
(Luke 2:19).

She wasn't unlike your daughter or sister or friend, a simple,
fun-loving girl, wondering about marriage, excited about the
future, content with a simple life in an ordinary village.

Mary loved the Lord, and she knew the Hebrew Scriptures
like the back of her hand. We know that because of her recorded

words in the Bible—especially her great prayer, the Magnificat, in Luke 1:46–55. It's so full of Old Testament references and quotations it sounds as if it were lifted directly from the Psalms or the writings of the prophets.

One day, when Mary was a young adult, perhaps as she fetched water from the well at the foot of Nazareth's hill, she turned and saw an angel. Not just any angel. It was Daniel's angel from the Old Testament. Or, more specifically, it was Israel's angel from the book of Daniel—the angel Gabriel. He addressed her as if she were the most important person in the world: "Greetings, you who are highly favored! The Lord is with you" (Luke 1:28).

Mary's heart jumped as Gabriel continued his message: "Do not be afraid, Mary; you have found favor with God. You will conceive and give birth to a son, and you are to call him Jesus" (Luke 1:30–31).

Gabriel shared incredible details about the birth of Israel's Messiah, and he answered Mary's questions with patience and insight. Then he came to his concluding sentence, recorded in Luke 1:37:

"For no word from God will ever fail."

What a claim! He didn't simply say that no message of God would fail, or that no chapter, paragraph, or sentence would fail.

Quick Tip: Many of our great hymns and praise songs are the products of someone who was meditating on a truth or verse of Scripture. Take a passage and convert it into your own song, poem, or prayer.

No, he said that not even a single *word* from God would ever fail to come to pass exactly as intended.

> Not even a single *word* from God would ever fail to come to pass exactly as intended.

Jesus said, "Heaven and earth will pass away, but my words will never pass away" (Matthew 24:35). God's Book is as infallible as His character, and His Word is worth treasuring up and pondering in our hearts. The Bible says, "For all of God's promises have been fulfilled in Christ with a resounding 'Yes!' And through Christ, our 'Amen' . . . ascends to God for his glory" (2 Corinthians 1:20 NLT).

Biblical meditation is treasuring up God's words and pondering them in our hearts. That's how Mary kept herself calm and prepared for the future. That's how she composed her spirit and withstood the plan of God and the pain of gossip. She pondered all these things—all God's words—in her heart.

Meditation Gives . . . Peace When the World Is Upended

Meditation provides peace when our world changes. Just last month at a conference, I attended a banquet. Making conversation,

I told my tablemates I was working on a book about biblical meditation. The woman to my right told me she had personally learned the power of meditation as a young adult. For her, it was a matter of pondering her problems in the light of Scripture.

"I believe God has placed His guiding hand on me throughout my life," she said.

When I was eleven, the Holy Spirit created a spirit in me to understand the truths of His Word. It began when a pastor visited our home with a Bible ministry on tape. I was interested in that; and from age eleven, I started listening to Bible tapes on an old reel-to-reel tape recorder. Each book of the Bible was taught, with interesting historical background and many valuable lessons. I heard many of the Bible verses over and over again, and to this day I can recite many of those verses by heart. I was also encouraged to memorize Scripture and to keep a Promise Notebook.

Well, in my early twenties, I faced a particular crisis and struggled to know what to do. I took many walks along a nearby river, and all those scriptures flowed through my mind like courses of water—that flood of Bible verses I'd learned in my childhood and teenage years.

It was as if the Holy Spirit was shouting the truth of Scripture at me, and I could do nothing to stop the flow of information, nor did I want to. There in my heart and mind and with each step along the riverbank, those verses brought guidance and truth.

I cannot say I always had peace in those moments, but I did have truth, and by meditating on these treasured passages, I found the wisdom and guidance I needed. We know from Scripture that God is no respecter of persons, but that He honors His Word wherever it's found. If it's in our hearts and minds, then He will honor His holy Word in us and bring blessing upon us.[1]

As she shared her story, I thought of Isaiah 30:21, which says, "Your ears shall hear a word behind you, saying, 'This is the way, walk in it,' whenever you turn to the right hand or whenever you turn to the left" (NKJV).

Meditation Gives . . . Energy When Work Is Unending

Meditation also inspires strength when our spirits falter or our work seems unending. Dr. Charles Stanley, in his book *How to Listen to God*, wrote:

> We can be tired, weary, and emotionally distraught, but after spending time alone with God, we find that He injects into our

bodies energy, power, and strength. God's spiritual dynamics are at work in our inner beings, refreshing and energizing our minds and spirits. There is nothing to match meditation in its impact upon our lives and the lives of others.[2]

In his autobiography, *Just As I Am*, Billy Graham recalled growing up on a North Carolina dairy farm. "Our barns had tin roofs," he wrote. . . .

On rainy days, I liked to sneak away into the hay barn and lie on a sweet-smelling and slippery pile of straw, listening to the raindrops hit that tin roof and dreaming. It was a sanctuary that helped shape my character. Whenever I visit a bustling city anywhere in the world now, I like to retreat from noisy boulevards into an open church building and just meditate in the cool, dim quietness. At our home in the Blue Ridge Mountains, my favorite spot is a little path above the house where I walk alone and talk with God.[3]

These quiet moments of prayer and meditation have often renewed the strength of kingdom workers like Mary of Nazareth, Charles Stanley, and Billy Graham. Their God is yours, too, and as you ponder His Word in your heart, you'll find energy for each day and strength for each task.

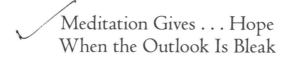

Meditation Gives . . . Hope
When the Outlook Is Bleak

Meditation gives hope in even our bleakest moments. Several years ago, while writing *The Lord Is My Shepherd*, I interviewed Maurice Pink, British World War II veteran who shared his experiences as a nineteen-year-old sailor when torpedoes struck his ship on December 10, 1941.

Maurice, three decks down, felt water crawling up his legs. He clambered up ladders and through passages, made it to the deck, stripped off his clothes, and jumped into the shark-infested South China Sea as the ship quickly sank. He felt disoriented, unsure of which way to swim, and he began to panic.

At that moment, he said, the Twenty-third Psalm came to mind. Treading water, he began quoting those words over and over. They were better than a life vest. They kept him unsinkable until the British destroyer HMS *Electra* rescued him an hour later.

"Would you like me to read what I've written about my experience?" he asked me.

There are times in your life when things don't go right and you feel all alone. That happened to me on December 10, 1941, when I was on the battle cruiser HMS *Repulse* with the nearby HMS *Prince of Wales*. We were attacked by the Japanese air force, which resulted in both ships being sunk. I found myself alone in the water, not able to see anyone else. It was then that the Twenty-third Psalm came into my head, and I realized I was not alone. I had a Shepherd. The Lord was my Shepherd; I did not need to want. I was not in green pastures, but in oily waters; but He restored my soul. Even though I was walking in the shadow of death, I was to fear no evil for He was with me.

The rod and staff did not ring a bell with me until voices above me were shouting. Looking up there was a big destroyer alongside me, HMS *Electra*, with nets over the side, which allowed me to climb up to safety. That was my rod and staff. I didn't have a table set before me, but I did get a cup of the ship's cocoa.

Since that day goodness and mercy have followed me all the days of my life, and when I think back to that day, I wonder what would have happened if I had died. There again, the psalm had the answer: I would dwell in the house of the Lord forever.

Thank you, Lord, for being my Shepherd and for the Twenty-third Psalm.[4]

That's meditation if I've ever heard it!

I've never been literally shipwrecked, but I have had times when things didn't go right and I've felt all alone. In such times I've often quoted Psalm 23, picturing its images and talking with its Good Shepherd. Once I slept fitfully on the sofa for several weeks because I couldn't relax in bed due to anxiety. Psalm 23 was my sleeping draught. I quoted it over and over, forcing my mind to focus on it rather than on my worries. I believe everyone on earth should know Psalm 23 by heart, because it can keep our heads above water when we feel overwhelmed.[5]

Meditation Gives . . .
Composure When Stress Is Great

Biblical meditation also gives composure when our nerves are stretched taut or we're stressed by other people.

Dr. Elmer Towns knew an office manager who liked everything about her job, except one thing. She didn't enjoy interacting with the plant manager. No matter what happened in the company, he was negative about it, and she dreaded being called into his office.

Dr. Towns suggested she meditate on the Lord's Prayer during such stressful moments. "Pray the Lord's Prayer on the way to his office," he said. The woman took up the challenge. Whenever she was called to the office, she silently pondered and prayed the Lord's Prayer along the way. By the time she arrived at his office, she was calm. Instead of being defensive and angry with him, she was able to say, "Let me help you get a better perspective."

She later said, "I got faith from the Lord's Prayer. It gave me courage to aggressively suggest new ways for him to look at things. Now I always say the Lord's Prayer walking from my desk to his office."[6]

The great thing about meditation is its privacy and portability. Without anyone knowing about it—even the person across the conference table from you—you can review a verse of Scripture or a passage such as the Lord's Prayer, running it through your brain like a bubbling brook.

Find God's best passages for your worst days—keep a list of them to refer to—and learn to calm yourself by massaging your mind with the oil of His Word.

Meditation Gives . . . Help When Resources Are Low

Biblical meditation helps us when our resources are low—whether time, energy, or even money. Here's a favorite example:

Dr. Frank Pollard, a far-famed name in Baptist circles, grew up in a broken-down environment in the Texas oil fields. His dad wanted him to be a lawyer, but when Frank decided to train for the ministry, his father refused to help finance his education. Frank left home in an old car with ten dollars in his pocket. A police officer stopped him for speeding. The fine was ten dollars.

"Then," said Frank, "I had no money and no place to stay overnight. It was getting late in the afternoon so I sat down, opened my Bible, and began to read. I turned to Matthew 6:33: 'Seek ye first the kingdom of God and his righteousness; and all these things shall be added unto you' (KJV)." Frank meditated on that. If God could take care of the birds and the weeds, could He not also care for His penniless child who had just lost his last ten dollars?

That evening Frank got a job selling soda pop at a Little League baseball game, and they paid him five dollars. He also ran into a friend who recruited him to work at the YMCA day camp, and part of the salary was free room and board.

"From that day forward," he said, "I have added 'Matthew 6:33' to my signature." He meditated on it all his life, and he never exhausted its meaning or power, for no word from God can ever fail.[7]

I've given these examples to show the practicality of biblical meditation. For the heroes of the Bible, meditation was a habit woven into the fabric of everyday life. Isaac meditated in the field. David meditated amidst the battles. Paul meditated in prison. Jesus meditated on the cross. Mary meditated by the well of Nazareth. And we can follow their examples.

Mary had a treasury of heaven-sent truth, and she pondered it in her heart. It gave her peace when her world was upended, energy when her work was unending, hope when her outlook was

Quick Tip: Remember that every verse only has one correct interpretation. We have to study the Bible to determine the meaning intended by the author of the passage. But every passage can have many applications. Study the context and strive to "rightly divide" the Word of God and to apply it wisely to your life.

bleak, composure when her stress was great, and help when her resources were low.

The same will happen to you as you learn to perpetually ponder God's Word in your heart.

For a free downloadable group study guide for this book as well as free personal audio meditation guides, visit www.robertjmorgan.com/meditation.

5

BIBLICAL MEDITATION:

Helping You Understand God's Word

Oh, how I love Your law!
It is my meditation all the day.

—PSALM 119:97 NKJV

When I was a boy I had a little record player that spun 45 rpm singles, which I kept stacked in a small rack. I spent hours listening to these timeless classics, dancing to them and singing "Zip-a-Dee-Doo-Dah," "You Are My Sunshine," and "The World Owes Me a Living." But sometimes the needle slipped out of its groove and slid back and forth across the vinyl, making a horrible noise and scratching my record. Only when it found its groove again did the music return.

I no longer have my little Victrola or my collection of records with their big holes in the center, but I still remember that horrible scratching sound. It goes off in my mind whenever the little needle in my soul gets out of its groove and rips across my nerves in a way that causes every part of me to either tense up or explode in anger.

Biblical meditation helps my mind find its groove again, and it provides the soundtrack for my life—songs of praise and melodies of joy based in Jesus.

When I'm struggling with patience as I help my disabled wife with some chore, it helps to whisper 1 Corinthians 13:4: "Love is patient, love is kind. It does not envy, it does not boast, it is not proud."

When I'm tempted to spend too much on a questionable purchase, Hebrews 13:5 is a great verse: "Keep your lives free from the love of money and be content with what you have."

When I'm troubled about my loved ones, I remember the words of Jesus in John 14:1: "Do not let your hearts be troubled. You believe in God; believe also in me."

When I get upset, I take a walk and remind myself of Proverbs 29:11: "Fools give full vent to their rage, but the wise bring calm in the end." (NIV)

When I'm envious of another's success, I think of the conversation between Peter and Jesus in John 21. Seeing the apostle

Quick Tip: Keep a meditation journal. Every day list the date and write down the verse or reference the Lord gives you. As you study the passage, jot down your thoughts about it. Over time, you'll develop your own informal Bible commentary.

John in the distance, Peter asked, "Lord, what about this man?" Jesus replied, "If I will that he remain till I come, what is that to you? You follow Me" (verses 21–22 NKJV).

When my sleep is hindered by miscellaneous worries about old age and death, it helps that I've memorized the opening of Revelation 21:1–2, "Then I saw 'a new heaven and a new earth,' for the first heaven and the first earth had passed away, and there was no longer any sea. I saw the Holy City, the new Jerusalem, coming down out of heaven from God, prepared as a bride beautifully dressed for her husband."

Whenever I've found myself in crisis—and, oh, how I hate crises!—the Word of God has never failed to provide a verse or passage to anchor my shifting emotions. Somehow, through meditation, I hear the Master's voice. Somehow through meditation, He lifts the wandering needle of my spirit and sets it again in the groove of His grace.

> There's nothing wrong with devotional books—I've written some myself—but they are to be supplements to our spiritual diet, not the main course.

To have mental access to these verses, we must be students of Scripture. Too many of us get our nourishment from devotional books, which are the results of the meditations of others. There's nothing wrong with devotional books—I've written some myself—but they are to be supplements to our spiritual diet, not the main course.

The same is true for commentaries. We rely too much on commentaries and not enough on contemplation. In our age of quick communication, we have come to expect all the information we need instantly. So when it comes to our biblical intake, we snatch a verse from an app, like day traders grabbing a donut on the way to the stock exchange.

True biblical meditation requires systematic Bible study, for the Word of God provides the fodder for further thinking. Let me suggest a fourfold plan for prayerfully approaching Scripture.

I. Read the Books of the Bible

First, try reading the Bible in book-sized units. When the Lord designed the Bible, He divided its contents into sixty-six units, which we call books, and each meets a different need in our lives. The contents of each book unfold logically, each paragraph based on the one preceding it, moving toward the great message God wants to give us in that particular book. By reading through the whole book, either in one sitting or over a period of time, we take in the panorama of its contents.

My friend Matt Gardner saw an interview with actor

Anthony Hopkins, who said that when he gets a movie script, he reads through it between one hundred and two hundred times before production. He makes notes in the margins. He scribbles and doodles and imagines how it would look on stage or screen. By the time Hopkins is finished, that script is internalized. He knows his character. He knows his (and everyone else's) lines. He's able to improvise, and he's a personification of the script.[1]

Matt told himself, "If a Hollywood actor reads a script a hundred times, why can't I read a book in the Bible a hundred times?"

He selected the book of James and started reading it over and over. James takes fewer than ten minutes to read. As Matt got into the project and the days passed, he began to see how certain themes emerged and repeated in the book. He began to get a sense of the author's personality and convictions. He became so familiar with this epistle he could think through it with his eyes closed, and he began looking at his everyday life through the practical lens of its contents.[2]

Perhaps you're overwhelmed with the thought of reading an entire book of the Bible, especially in one sitting. I've conducted a personal experiment of how long it takes. Most of the books can be read in just a few minutes. It took me ten minutes to read Lamentations; four minutes to read Jonah; seventeen minutes to read 2 Corinthians; eleven minutes for Galatians; and one minute to cover every word of 2 John.

The longer books I sometimes tackle on overseas flights or when I'm at the beach. I read Genesis in an hour and thirty-seven minutes. Exodus took an hour and fifteen minutes. Matthew took fifty-two minutes, less time than my favorite hour-long television drama.

But don't feel you have to sit down and read the whole book of Psalms, for example, at once. Just read it systematically. If you read a psalm a day, for example, you'll work through the whole book in 150 days. In just five months you'll emerge from your study with a heart of praise.

If you prayerfully select a shorter book, like James or Philippians, and read it over and over, you'll better grasp the chain of logic God embedded into that book. You'll increase in wisdom as Scripture molds your mind. God's sixty-six love letters to you will begin transforming your thinking, your attitudes, and your actions.

2. Study the Passages of the Bible

It's also helpful to study the Bible in smaller bites, drilling into paragraphs, sentences, and words, looking at each in context. In David W. Saxton's book about meditation, he suggests believers "must choose a small enough verse or theme that enables detailed concentration."[3]

Sometimes in my daily devotions, I'll read a larger portion of Scripture—all five chapters of James, for instance. But on other days I'll devote my time to just one paragraph in James, or maybe just one verse. For example, recently while reading through James, I spent several days on James 1:2–3, which begins: "Consider it pure joy, my brothers and sisters, whenever you face trials of many kinds." That's counterintuitive to our normal reactions in life, but the next word is "because," and then James goes on to list reasons to be joyful amid trials. I found it therapeutic to bullet-point his list and study each line of his thinking.

There's so much you can do with a paragraph of Scripture. You can read it, dissect it, diagram it, outline it, paraphrase it, condense it, take it apart, put it back together, check its cross-references, study its words, and list its applications. You can sing it, shout it, pray it.

The Bible is inexhaustible in its wisdom and in its application. Every time we open its cover, we find something fresh and new, even in familiar texts. God has given us a book small enough to hold in our hands, big enough to study for a lifetime, and rich enough to satisfy our hearts and minds forever.

Find a good study Bible with an introduction to each book and some commentary on the verses. Think of yourself as a life-long student of Scripture. Make it a part of your routine. Find a time and place to study, a desk or table. Grab a notebook and pen. Underline. Highlight. Circle. Ponder. Personalize. Build it into each day's agenda.

Become acquainted with God's Word, with all its books and paragraphs and verses, with all its commands and claims, with all its precepts and promises, for, as Deuteronomy 32:47 says: "They are not just idle words for you—they are your life."

> God has given us a book small enough to hold in our hands, big enough to study for a lifetime, and rich enough to satisfy our hearts and minds forever.

3. Digest the Thoughts of the Bible

My friend Sam Doherty, who began the work of Child Evangelism Fellowship in Ireland, tells of a fearful time in his life. His only son, Stephen, developed severe health problems and needed a liver transplant. He waited for two years, growing weaker all the time. Sam became increasingly concerned, but the Lord gave him a verse to meditate on—Psalm 91:15: "He will call on me, and I will answer him; I will be with him in trouble." Sam took that as a personal promise from God and it strengthened him greatly. But one day, his faith faltered just a bit, and Sam asked God to confirm that promise in a more definite way. That very morning,

Sam's regular Bible reading was in Psalm 99. As he read verse 6, he realized it had his own name in it: "Samuel was among those who called on his name; they called on the LORD, and he answered them." Sam later said, "When I saw my name, I realized that I couldn't get any promise more definite or clear than that."[4]

When I read Sam's story, I thought of something Ruth Bell Graham wrote in her book *It's My Turn.* As a young girl, Ruth was sent to boarding school in Korea, and she was lonely and confused. In desperation, she went to her sister, Rosa, for advice. "I don't know what to tell you to do," said Rosa, "unless you take some verse and put your own name in it. See if that helps."[5]

In a sense, meditation is finding verses in the Bible and putting our names in them. It is pondering and personalizing Scripture. As you read through the books in the Bible, study its paragraphs and memorize some of its key verses, you'll find that meditation begins happening almost automatically. As you fall in love with God's Book, you'll think about it more—and you'll think about *Him* more. The Holy Spirit will bring verses to mind just as you need them, and meditation will become a natural and ongoing mental habit.

There is a little booklet by the Navigators that set me on the path of meditation decades ago. The writer suggested that our meditating on Scripture is similar to a cow chewing its cud.

Meditation is pondering various thoughts by mulling them over in the mind and heart. It is the processing of mental food. We might call it "thought digestion." Chewing upon a thought deliberately and thoroughly, thus providing a vital link between theory and action. What metabolism is to the physical body of a cow, meditation is to your mental and spiritual life.[6]

In much the same way as our bodies crave physical food, our spirits crave spiritual food. Biblical meditation enables us to begin consuming and digesting the thoughts of the Bible.

- The prophet Jeremiah said, "Your words were found, and I ate them, and Your word was to me the joy and rejoicing of my heart" (Jeremiah 15:16 NKJV).
- Job said, "I have treasured the words of his mouth more than my daily bread" (Job 23:12).
- The Psalmist said, "How sweet are your words to my taste" (Psalm 119:103).
- Jesus said, "Man shall not live on bread alone, but on every word that comes from the mouth of God" (Matthew 4:4).

Reading and hearing the Bible is like eating it—it enters into our bodies, our spirits. When we meditate on what we've read and heard, we're chewing and digesting the material until it's assimilated into our systems, disseminated throughout our personalities, and actually becomes *us*.

In Luke 24, Jesus joined two of His disciples as they trekked from Jerusalem to Emmaus. It was the afternoon of the first Easter, and the two were perplexed by the brutal death of their Messiah and the puzzling rumors of His resurrection. They heard footsteps behind them, and a mysterious Stranger drew near and engaged them in conversation. He listened to their queries and began telling them what they yearned to know. "And beginning with Moses and all the Prophets, he explained to them what was said in all the Scriptures concerning himself" (Luke 24:27). After arriving at their home and breaking bread with them, Jesus vanished from sight. But later, as the two disciples discussed their never-to-be-forgotten walk, they said, "Were not our hearts burning within us while he talked with us on the road and opened the Scriptures to us?" (verse 32). Verse 45 goes on to say that Jesus "opened their minds so they could understand the Scripture."

> Reading and hearing the Bible is like eating it—it enters into our bodies, our spirits.

Notice how Jesus *opened the Scriptures* to their minds and He *opened their minds* to the Scripture. What Jesus did for them, the Holy Spirit does for us. The apostle Paul said, "We have received, not the spirit of the world, but the Spirit who is from God, that we might know the things that have been freely given to us by God" (I Corinthians 2:12 NKJV).[7]

Bible study was never meant to be merely academic. It's relational. Transformational. It's not simply studying a book; it's fellowshipping with a Friend.

4. Share the Message of the Bible

Once we've read and studied and digested the Word, then we're ready to share its message. Notice that meditation—reading, studying, and digesting—is a prerequisite to passing along God's Word to others. Too many preachers and teachers rush from revelation to relevance without taking time for reflection. Too often we rush from our *text* to our *talk* without taking time for *thought*. But Psalm 39:3 says, "While I meditated, the fire burned; then I spoke with my tongue."

In my own experience, I've found I cannot effectively go straight from Bible study to sermon preparation. I need time to think through the material, often during long walks in the park or pacing around my backyard. My best insights come when I'm actually away from my desk, meditating on what I've learned. I frequently stop to jot down my thoughts and ideas, which I later hammer into sermons, like a blacksmith when his iron is hot.

In his little booklet on the life of Jonathan Edwards, Ed Reese wrote:

One of the secrets of [Edwards's] success was that he always thought through his subject matter. Even on walks and while riding horseback through the woods, he would jot down items and pin them to his coat. When he returned to the parsonage, he wrote out the fuller explanation of the bits noted on the scraps. It is said that at times the whole of his coat front would sometimes be covered with bits and pieces of paper.[8]

Remember this little poem from childhood?

As I walk'd by myself,
I talk'd to myself,
and myself replied to me;
And the questions myself
then put to myself,
with their answers I gave to thee.[9]

Biblical meditation is the art of talking to ourselves about what God has told us; and what we share with others is the overflow.

If you commit yourself to the habit of reading the books of the Bible, studying its passages, digesting its thoughts, and sharing its secrets with others, you'll find your groove—and the truth of God's Word will provide a praiseworthy soundtrack for life.

For a free downloadable group study guide for this book as well as free personal audio meditation guides, visit www.robertjmorgan.com/meditation.

6

BIBLICAL MEDITATION:

Gaining Insight into God's Will

And we all, who with unveiled faces contemplate
the Lord's glory, are being transformed into his
image with ever-increasing glory, which comes
from the Lord, who is the Spirit.

—2 CORINTHIANS 3:18

I recently pondered Jeremiah 23, a chapter in which the Lord condemned the false prophets who deceived the people of Judah. These bogus preachers claimed to have a message from God. "But which of them has *stood in the council of the LORD* to see or to hear his word?" asked verse 18 (emphasis mine).

A bit later, the Lord said, "I did not speak to them, yet they have prophesied. But if they had *stood in my council*, they would have proclaimed my words to my people" (verses 21–22, emphasis mine).

I was struck by the concept of *standing in the council of the Lord*. As a Bible teacher, I've wondered what that looks like and feels like. In my mind, this is how I picture it:

> Sitting at a table with my opened Bible, I see myself, as it were, approaching a vast domed archive. It's a treasury built of the finest Makrana marble, gleaming and grand, sitting in the center of a manicured estate.
>
> Pressing through lacquered doors, I enter the rotunda and find myself in a vast library. Thin windows of beveled glass look out onto green meadows and still waters. High above, a golden dome anchors a chandelier. Between the windows are towering shelves filled with leather volumes. The room is richly paneled in gleaming wood, and a tall desk stands at its center.
>
> I've entered the world's most perfect library, and every volume is at my disposal. But there are only sixty-six books. Climbing a ladder, I reach up and grab Genesis, or Ruth, or Psalms, or Proverbs. The prophets occupy adjacent shelves. Nearby are Matthew, Mark, Luke, and John. Across the way are the epistles of Paul. On the next shelves are James, Jude, Hebrews, and Peter. Occupying a spot on a shelf by itself is Revelation, held upright by bookends of marble cherubim.
>
> Grabbing one of the volumes, I take it to the desk in the center

of the room. Opening the book, I begin to read, each word flaming into gold as my eyes fall upon it. I remember, then, what I saw engraved in the marble of the entranceway:

> *The law of the LORD is perfect, refreshing the soul.*
> *The statutes of the LORD are trustworthy, making wise the simple.*
> *The precepts of the LORD are right, giving joy to the heart.*
> *The commands of the LORD are radiant, giving light to the eyes . . .*
> *They are more precious than gold.*
>
> PSALM 19:7–8, 10

Even as my visit draws to a close, and I return the book its shelf and leave the archives, I don't leave the words behind, for they've been transcribed onto the walls of my own internal library. I take them with me to ponder, to picture, to personalize, to practice, to preach.

This, to me, is standing in the council of God, the Wonderful Counselor who promised, "I will instruct you and teach you in the way you should go; I will counsel you with my loving eye on you" (Psalm 32:8).

You don't have to be a preacher to try this, or a professional scholar. The other day I came across my granddaughter at a table by the window. She was reading and taking notes on a pad of paper.

Quick Tip: Invest in a good study Bible with introductions to each of the sixty-six books, cross-references in the margins, and maps in the back. Don't be afraid to underline and highlight it. When a verse speaks to you in a memorable way, jot the date beside it as a record of God's message to your heart.

"What are you doing?" I asked.

"I'm having my quiet time, Papa," she said. "I'm studying the Bible."

Later I passed the table and saw her notes. She had taken a verse from the book of Proverbs and dissected it and analyzed it, just as I would do if I were preparing a sermon. She had devoured that verse. She had been standing in the council of God.

As we frequent this majestic library, making it a regular stop on each day's schedule and fellowshipping with its eternal Curator, we'll gain insight into God's will for our lives. We'll have wisdom for each day's trials and tasks.

Psalm 119 uses the word *meditation* to describe how this wondrous process works. The writer said (emphasis added):

- "I *meditate* on your precepts and consider your ways" (verse 15).
- "Though rulers sit together and slander me, your servant will *meditate* on your decrees" (verse 23).
- "Cause me to understand the way of your precepts, that I may *meditate* on your wonderful deeds" (verse 27).
- "I reach out for your commands, which I love, that I may *meditate* on your decrees" (verse 48).
- "I will *meditate* on your precepts" (verse 78).

- "Oh, how I love your law! I *meditate* on it all day long" (verse 97).
- "I have more insight than all my teachers, for I *meditate* on your statutes" (verse 99).
- "My eyes stay open through the watches of the night, that I may *meditate* on your promises" (verse 148).

"My Heart Meditated and My Spirit Asked"

One of the best biblical illustrations of using meditation to gain insight into God's Word comes from Asaph, the author of Psalms 77 and 78. We find him in Psalm 77 terribly anxious, so distraught that he couldn't sleep: "At night I stretched out untiring hands, and I would not be comforted" (verse 2).

How often does fear steal our sleep? Fear is like a skeletal hand that reaches into our chests, squeezing our hearts. This bony hand has many sharp fingers—anxiety, worry, anger, depression, obsession, compulsion, discouragement, jealousy, foreboding, phobia, timidity, mistrust, and that nagging sense of unease.

When Asaph found himself unable to sleep, caught in the clutches of fear and worry, he meditated:

I remembered you, God. . . . I meditated . . . I thought about the former days, the years of long ago . . . My heart meditated and my spirit asked. (verses 3–6)

In his meditations he asked himself some questions and pondered the answers:

"Will the Lord reject forever? Will he never show his favor again? Has his unfailing love vanished forever? Has his promise failed for all time? Has God forgotten to be merciful?" (verses 7–9)

Then Asaph began answering his own questions by reviewing God's faithfulness in the past. He wrote in verses 10–12:

Then I thought, "To this I will appeal: the years when the Most High stretched out his right hand. I will remember the deeds of the LORD; yes, I will remember your miracles of long ago. I will consider all your works and meditate on your mighty deeds."

As Asaph pondered God's Word, He meditated on God Himself, and that's the key. Biblical meditation isn't just a matter of meditating on Scripture; it's meditating on the God of Scripture. Beyond the sacred page, we see the Lord. It's not just the Word *Itself*, but the Word *Himself*, the Incarnate Word.

> Biblical meditation isn't just a matter of meditating on Scripture; it's meditating on the God of Scripture.

We're to meditate on the essence, the personality, the holiness, the faithfulness, the changelessness, the goodness, the greatness, the power, the love, the majesty, and the grace of our God.

We're to contemplate the incomprehensible, see the invisible, ponder the imponderable, and marvel at the mystery of Him who is the Three-in-One and One-yet-Three. He is the Ancient of Days, whose comings and goings are from old, even from everlasting.

We're to think about Him who formed the mountains, filled the seas, and flung the stars across the sky. His throne occupies the highest spot of the highest heaven, far above all rule and authority, power and dominion, and every name that is named, both in the present age and in the one to come. He is to be feared and followed, loved and obeyed, praised and worshipped.

He is the God of Abraham, Isaac, and Jacob; the God of our fathers, the God of Israel, the God of glory, the God of hope, the God of peace, and the God of the ages.

He is the One God who is able to keep us from falling, able to do more than we can ask or imagine, able to present us faultless before the throne, able to make all grace abound to us so that at all times—having all that we need—we will abound in every good work.

He is our best thought by day or by night.

In Psalm 77, Asaph continued,

Your ways, God, are holy. What god is as great as our God? You are the God who performs miracles; you display your power among the peoples. (verses 13–14)

Pondering this, Asaph recalled the parting of the Red Sea:

The waters saw you, God . . . The very depths were convulsed . . . Your path led through the sea, your way through the mighty waters, though your footprints were not seen. You led your people like a flock. (verses 16, 19–20)

As I wrote in my book *The Red Sea Rules*, Asaph realized the "Red Sea may roll before us; the desert may entrap us; the enemy may press on our heels. The past may seem implausible and the future impossible, but God works in ways we cannot see. . . . God will always make a way for His tired, yet trusting children, even if He must split the sea to do it."[1]

By the time we get to the next Psalm, Asaph had recovered

from his terrible night, and his personal meditations have become a public sermon. Psalm 78 opens:

> My people, hear my teaching; listen to the words of my mouth. . . .
> We will tell the next generation the praiseworthy deeds of the
> Lord. (verses 1, 4)

Think on These Things

The apostle Paul knew how to stand in the council of God. I love his meditations in the book of Philippians, written while he was imprisoned, chained, deprived of life's necessities, separated from his loved ones, and uncertain about his future. Yet this little letter to the church at Philippi rings with brightness, joy, contentment, vision, enthusiasm, confidence, and thanksgiving. His attitude was determined by his thinking, and his thinking was formed by meditating on the truths of the God whom he served. He advised the Philippians:

> Finally, brothers and sisters, whatever is true, whatever is noble,
> whatever is right, whatever is pure, whatever is lovely, whatever is
> admirable—if anything is excellent or praiseworthy—think about
> such things. Whatever you have learned or received or heard from

me, or seen in me—put it into practice. And the God of peace will be with you. (Philippians 4:8–9)

This is the universal experience of God's people and the unfailing practice of biblical heroes from Genesis to Revelation. Our pressures drive us to His principles. His principles lead us to His person. By meditating on His principles and person, we persevere through our struggles and arrive at praise. Then we have a message to preach to others.

It's hard today to find quiet zones to meditate on His promises. But moments of meditation are necessary to restore our souls, as Asaph found on that fearful night long ago and as Paul learned in the darkness of his prison cell.

We have to process our emotions, which takes time; but biblical meditation has a way of turning our attention from the problems we face to the face of the God we serve. Biblical meditation is therapy for the soul, heaven's medication. And through this process we come to understand God's good, perfect, and pleasing will.

So learn to stand in the council of the Lord. It's the most exclusive privilege in the universe. The Bible says, "We have gained access" (Romans

> Biblical meditation has a way of turning our attention from the problems we face to the face of the God we serve.

5:2). Because of Christ, you'll never be denied entrance, and His library never closes.

Think on these things, meditate on them, and Psalm 119:105 will be true for you:

> Your word is a lamp for my feet, a light on my path.

For a free downloadable group study guide for this book as well as free personal audio meditation guides, visit www.robertjmorgan.com/meditation.

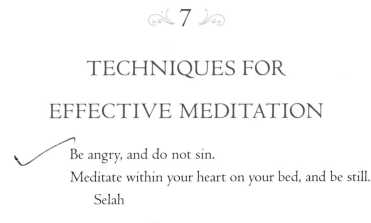

7

TECHNIQUES FOR

EFFECTIVE MEDITATION

Be angry, and do not sin.
Meditate within your heart on your bed, and be still.
Selah

—Psalm 4:4 nkjv

After thirty-six years as senior pastor, I recently told my church I needed to shift roles. I wasn't resigning or retiring, but my circumstances no longer allowed me to bear the full load of leadership.

On Saturday before making the announcement, I was jittery. I didn't know how people would react, and my stomach was knotted. That evening I found a spot where I could lean back, close my eyes, breathe rhythmically, and recite Scripture to myself. I quoted one passage after another, going through my memory verses. My jitters begin to fall away like leaves from an autumn tree, and the next day I stood in the pulpit as relaxed as if standing in my own backyard with my grandkids.

To me, meditation is that simple—something to be incorporated into our days like a thread of gold into a tapestry. In this chapter, I want to give concrete examples to encourage you to come up with your own methods of biblical meditation.

Meditate When You Awaken

I recently attended an event in Washington, D.C., and met Nobel Peace Prize winner Lord David Trimble, who helped broker the Belfast Agreement on Good Friday of 1998. During one of the breaks, I talked to him about meditation, and, without hesitation, he told me that he meditates in a definite way on two occasions.

The first is when he attends his Presbyterian church on Sunday mornings, because, he said, he listens intently as the Scripture is explained in its context. His pastor's weekly sermon anchors his personal Bible study and his meditation for the coming week.

Then, Trimble said, every morning when he awakens, he rests in bed as sunlight filters into the room. He thinks and prays and

Quick Tip: Keep a Bible with you and read it at odd moments. The other day at the lake, I saw a young lifeguard sitting under an umbrella during his break, poring over a book with a highlighter. Turns out, he was studying the book of Daniel, soaking in the message of the Bible the way the guests around him were soaking in the sun. It's handy to have an electronic version on your mobile device, but sometimes the old-fashioned printed page gives us a literal feel for the Word.

ponders. He mulls over his day, seeking guidance for his agenda. His best ideas, he told me, come to him before he ever gets up. By the time he rises, he's ready to plunge into the day with energy and cheerfulness.

Samuel Logan Brengle said, "If you would redeem the time, begin the moment your eyes open in the morning. Let no idle, foolish, hurtful thoughts be harbored for an instant, but begin at once to pray and praise God and to meditate on His glories, His goodness and faithfulness and truth, and your heart will soon burn within you and bubble over with joy."[1]

This was the habit of the writer of Psalm 143:8:

> Let the morning bring me word of your unfailing love, for I have put my trust in you. Show me the way I should go, for to you I entrust my life.

Beginning the morning with even a few moments of quiet, biblical meditation sets the tone for the rest of the day. But in our busy, rushing lives even those few moments can slip away from us as we hurry to begin the day's checklist of activities. In fact, I've read that most people spend little time thinking; and when they do, it's while showering, driving, or exercising. And actually, the morning shower is an excellent time to meditate. Unless you have waterproof speakers, you're probably free from noise. Unless you shower at the gym, you probably have privacy. The soap, shampoo, hot water, and steam create a perfect meditation zone if you're intentional about it; otherwise your mind will go to some problem, appointment, obligation, or aggravation. But try this: Tomorrow take a Bible verse into the shower along with your soap and washcloth. Rinse off your mind. Train yourself to ponder a truth of Scripture while you go about your scrubbing and shampooing.

Meditate During Daily Time with the Lord

When I asked Bible teacher Kay Arthur when she meditates, she told me that her meditation is grounded in her daily Bible study. "Sometimes while reading my Bible during my quiet time, I'm so moved by a truth or fact I've seen—the fact that God is sovereign over all the circumstances of life—I just pick up my open Bible and bring it to my chest and close my eyes and thank God for speaking to me."

"Whenever I open the Book," she continued,

> Tomorrow take a Bible verse into the shower along with your soap and washcloth. Rinse off your mind.

I'm looking at the very words God wrote, so I am immersing myself in God's truth. I'm sitting down and listening to what God wants to tell me, what He wants me to know. He's giving me the knowledge I need, which is something Peter talked about over and over in his second epistle: "Grace and peace be yours in abundance through the *knowledge* of God and of Jesus our Lord. His divine power has given us everything we need for a godly life through our *knowledge* of Him who called us . . . For this very reason, make every effort to add . . . *knowledge* . . . For if you possess these qualities in increasing measure, they will keep you from being ineffective and unproductive in your *knowledge* of our Lord Jesus Christ. . . . But grow in the grace and *knowledge* of our Lord and Savior Jesus Christ." [2 Peter 1:2–8, 3:18, emphasis mine]

In my book, *Mastering Life Before It's Too Late*, I devote a section to Bible study, prayer, meditation, and day planning. Whether it's in the morning, or at noon or night, build time into your daily routine—find your quiet place, read His Word, absorb His knowledge, and talk to your Father in secret.

Meditate as You Drive

One Sunday in 1974, my friend Reese Kauffman of Child Evangelism Fellowship heard an evangelist say, "Tomorrow when you drive to work, take your right hand and turn the knob to the left and spend time talking with God." Reese realized the evangelist was telling the crowd to turn off their radios when driving to work the next morning so they could spend time in fellowship with the Lord.

The next morning Reese got into his Pontiac and turned the radio off. He spent his drive time talking with the Lord and meditating on Scripture. At the end of that afternoon, he felt the day had been different. Walking to his car to return home, he decided to continue the experiment.

"After all," he observes, "how a man enters his house at night sets the tone for his family. If we walk through the door exhausted and exasperated and carrying the burdens of the day, we'll transfer that to our families. But it's different if we drive home saying, 'Now the most important part of my day is coming home, being with my wife, with my children, I'll just pray about that.'"

In this way, Reese learned to turn his commuting time into communing time.[2]

Some of my best thinking is also done while driving. If I get writer's block, sometimes I jump in the car and drive the loop around my city, thinking about the biblical passage I'm dealing with. Somewhere along the route, I inevitably pull over and start making notes because of fresh thoughts flowing into my mind.

Quick Tip: Frame and
hang beautifully inscribed
Bible verses on the walls
of your home. They'll
be a reminder to you, an
inspiration to your children
and family, and a silent
witness to your guests.

Meditate on the Plane

Include meditation material in your carry-on when flying. Some of my best ideas have come at 35,000 feet. In the late 1990s, I was flying home from Athens, torn apart with anxiety. I had a window seat and, thankfully, no seatmate. I lowered my tray table, got out my notepad and Bible, and resumed my regular Bible reading from the day before. I was in Exodus 14, the story of the Israelites at the Red Sea. My meditations spilled onto my notepad, and from that experience came ten personal rules for handling difficulties—*The Red Sea Rules.*

I fly quite a bit, and I'm usually stuffed into a window seat in tourist class. But if I have my earphones with ocean waves, my Bible, and my little notebook, I can often use the high altitudes to think through biblical passages and to meditate on a higher plane, so to speak.

Meditate When You Close Your Eyes a Moment

When he was emperor, Napoleon would sometimes stretch out on the settee near the fireplace and appear to be dozing. But his aides soon learned he was meditating. He explained:

If I always seem to be ready for everything, to face up to anything, it is because I never undertake anything at all without first having meditated for a long time and foreseen what might happen. It is not a genie, but meditation, that suddenly reveals to me, in secret, what I must say or do under circumstances not anticipated by others.[3]

Just as Napoleon meditated on his battles, we must meditate on our Bibles. Often before an obligation, I'll stretch out in the recliner, close my eyes, and let my mind review the scriptures I've been studying. It seems to prepare me for whatever comes.

Meditate When You Behold the Glories of God's Creation

Rosalind Goforth, missionary to China, wrote of walking in the country with her elderly father, who was an artist. One evening he stopped and plucked a single violet.

He remained examining it for so long that I became impatient and said, "Father, dear, do come on." Gently he laid a restraining hand on mine as he said, almost in a tone of awe, "Child, just look at the exquisite beauty of this tiny flower—its color and delicate tracery! Oh, how wonderful it is!" As we started on, he exclaimed, with deep feeling, speaking as if to himself, "What a wonderful artist God is!"[4]

We don't have to travel to a national park or hike along the Appalachian Trail to meditate on the wonders of God's creation. A single blossom will do, if we'll just take time to smell the roses, consider the lilies, hear the crickets, and drink in the sunsets.

Meditate When You Walk

In his book *On Writing*, novelist Stephen King described a particular project that gave him fits. He couldn't resolve a difficult issue with the plot of one of his stories, and he almost gave up. Rather than abandoning the novel, he started taking long walks. "I spent those walks being bored and thinking about my gigantic boondoggle of a manuscript," he said.

> For weeks I got exactly nowhere in my thinking—it just seemed too hard. . . . I circled the problem again and again, beat my fists on it, knocked my head against it . . . and then one day when I was thinking of nothing much at all, the answer came to me. It arrived whole and complete—gift-wrapped, you could say—in a single bright flash. I ran home and jotted it down on paper, the only time I've done such a thing, because I was terrified of forgetting."[5]

I'm not a fan of Mr. King's novels, but I am a fan of his method of taking meditation walks. As I mentioned earlier, many a thought bounces around in my brain as my footsteps amble through the greenways or along the mountain trails.

Meditate When You Feel Lonely

Samuel Logan Brengle traveled incessantly for the Lord and often found himself in empty hotel rooms at night. "I am a lonely man," he wrote,

> . . . and yet I am not lonely. With my open Bible I live with prophets, priests, and kings; I walk and hold communion with apostles, saints, martyrs, and with Jesus, and mine eyes see the King in His beauty and the land that is afar off. . . . My daily reading has brought me into company with the great prophets—Isaiah, Jeremiah, Ezekiel, Hosea, Micah, Malachi, and others—and I live again with them in the midst of the throbbing, tumultuous, teeming life of old Jerusalem, Samaria, Egypt, and Babylon. These prophets are old friends of mine. . . . They have blessed me a thousand times, kindled in me some of the flaming zeal for righteous, their scorn for meanness, duplicity, pride, and worldliness. . . . I have for many years lived with St. Paul. Far more constantly and intimately than

he lived and traveled with his friend Barnabas and his young lieu-
tenants, has he lived, traveled, slept, and talked with me.

Brengle's habit of meditation was to find verses in the morning as his texts for the day and to think about them all day long.
His biographer likened it to a man stuffing his pockets with
snacks to enjoy throughout the day.[6]

Meditate When You Awaken in the Night

Psalm 119:148 says, "My eyes stay open through the watches of
the night, that I may meditate on your promises."

Is that sometimes true for you?

I was quite discouraged as I prepared for bed last night,
and I jotted a few plaintive words in my journal. I'm looking at
them now. "I am discouraged and overwhelmed," I had written.
"Worked much of the day on a project, and took a six-mile walk
on the greenway to think it through, but didn't get it done. Stuck.
Worried I'm not spending enough time with grandkids. Tired.
Lord, I need help."

Then I thumbed through the pages of my mind and thought
of Psalm 121. I resolved to fall asleep thinking about that psalm.
I recall waking up several times, quoting, "I will lift up my eyes

to the hills—from whence comes my help? My help comes from the LORD, who made heaven and earth" (verses 1–2 NKJV). My mood was considerably better this morning.

Dawson Trotman, founder of the Navigators, believed the last prevailing thought in one's conscious mind before going to sleep should be some portion of God's Word. He called this his H.W.L.W. Principle (His Word the Last Word). He felt the last dominant idea would simmer in the subconscious and become the first thought on rising.[7]

These are some of the tips and techniques that I have found to be useful; you can certainly add your own. Meditation is very personal and practical. You can do it whenever, wherever, however you'd like. It's essentially finding quiet moments to ponder the Lord and His Word and to realign your thinking so that it corresponds with His Truth.

We meditate as we pray, as we sing praises to God, as we worship, as we witness, as we compose songs or sermons or articles or Bible lessons, as we talk with others about the Word of God, as we listen, as we delight in the Word of the Lord day and night.

The one who learns to do this—the one like you—will be

> The last prevailing thought in one's conscious mind before going to sleep should be some portion of God's Word.

"like a tree planted by streams of water, which yields its fruit in season and whose leaf does not wither" (Psalm 1:3).

Psalm 1 begins with the perfect word to describe such a person: *blessed!*

For a free downloadable group study guide for this book as well as free personal audio meditation guides, visit www.robertjmorgan.com/meditation.

8

FINDING GODLY

SUCCESS GOD'S WAY

Then those who feared the Lord spoke to
one another, and the Lord listened and
heard them; so a book of remembrance was
written before Him for those who fear the
Lord and who meditate on His name.

—Malachi 3:16 nkjv

J. I. Packer's classic book, *Knowing God,* was published when I
was a pliable college student, and his words molded my mind
like clay. Reading it, I realized that while it's vital to hammer out
truthful doctrines and sound convictions, we shouldn't merely be
academic believers in God or in His Word. We learn the *Truth*

of God so we can better know the *God of Truth,* and a primary way that happens is through meditation.

Packer wrote:

> How can we turn our knowledge *about* God into knowledge *of* God? The rule for doing this is demanding, but simple. It is that we turn each truth that we learn about God into a matter for meditation before God, leading to prayer and praise to God.[1]

About the time I was reading Packer's book, I noticed something in my own study of the Bible, and it convinced me that my life would be a guaranteed success if I learned and practiced this habit of biblical meditation. That's not as boastful as it sounds. Even as a young adult, I knew God's view of success might not equate with fame, fortune, or prestige. I was a shy young man, battling low self-esteem, and ill prepared for manhood, marriage, or a meaningful career. Still, my study of three special passages in the Bible persuaded me that success—as God meant it—was available and, indeed, inevitable, if I simply embraced the lost art of biblical meditation.

I want to show you these passages. You'll find them near the beginning, in the middle, and near the end of the Bible.

Commands and Promises

The first passage is Joshua 1:8:

> "Keep this Book of the Law always on your lips; meditate on it day and night, so that you may be careful to do everything written in it. Then you will be prosperous and successful."

This verse contains three commands and two promises. The commands: (1) we're to keep the Scripture on our lips—reading it, speaking it, quoting it; (2) we must meditate on it day and night; and (3) we must practice it, being careful to do what it says.

The promises: (1) then you will be prosperous, and (2) you will have success.

God appeared to Joshua after the death of Moses to tell him how to lead the Israelites into the promised land. It was a time of dramatic transition. There were battles ahead, and the Israelites were on the verge of fulfilling a dream that reached back to the days of Abraham. They were about to occupy their God-promised homeland.

What kind of training did God give Joshua? At this critical moment, what discussions took place?

"They did not discuss military strategies or battle plans at this rare meeting," wrote David Saxton. "Rather, the Lord told Joshua that his greatest need was to live by meditating upon God's word."[2]

If you think about it, it makes perfect sense. Our fallen minds are futile. Without the insights that come from God and His Word, our thoughts never really get out of the basement of life. When we learn to meditate day and night on Scripture, God uses that practice to rewire our brains. Meditation elevates our moods. It fills us with God's thoughts, which are always successful. We begin to see things as He does, and the inevitable result is success.

But it's success as God defines it. A joyful life that bears fruit. Purpose. Perseverance. Pleasantness. Faithfulness. Godliness. Cheerfulness. Holiness. Hopefulness. Everlasting life. Friendship with God.

Whatever They Do Prospers

The second passage is Psalm 1, which was almost certainly written by David as a sort of verbal painting of Joshua 1:8. It begins:

> Blessed is the one who does not walk in step with the wicked or
>
> stand in the way that sinners take or sit in the company of mockers,

but whose delight is in the law of the LORD, and who meditates on his law day and night. That person is like a tree planted by streams of water, which yields its fruit in season and whose leaf does not wither—whatever they do prospers. (verses 1–3)

Notice the similar command: the blessed person is the one who meditates on the law of the Lord day and night.

Notice the similar promise: Whatever they do prospers.

The difference is in the imagery, and that brings up an important point: imagery is a critical component of meditation. God gave us minds capable of imagination, capable of dreaming, of daydreaming, of fantasizing, of seeing pictures and portraits and movies in our heads. We can paint and hang pictures on the walls of our mind.

By nature, our brains choose to scrawl worthless graffiti, but meditation colors and fills our minds with masterpieces. If we harness the power of imagination, we can accomplish remarkable things.

On a certain level, today's best athletes know this, which is why major sports teams hire psychologists. The Brazilian soccer star Pelé credited much of his success to visualizing his games in advance. Before every game,

> By nature, our brains choose to scrawl worthless graffiti, but meditation colors and fills our minds with masterpieces.

Pelé arrived at the stadium earlier than necessary. Finding a quiet spot, he lay down, covered his eyes with a towel, and watched a kind of mental movie of his life. He saw himself as a kid playing soccer on the beach. He felt the sun on his back and the breeze in his hair. He reviewed some of his greatest moments in the sport, letting himself feel and enjoy their intensity as if they were occurring in real time.

Then he saw himself racing into that day's game, seeing the crowds, hearing the cheers, and watching himself play at peak performance, dribbling, kicking, darting, dashing, scoring. By the time Pelé jogged onto the field, he had already won the game in his mind.[3]

I believe David applied similar imagination to Joshua 1. Perhaps one day while watching his flocks, he sat on a rock and pondered Joshua 1:8, which he had probably memorized. He may have thought to himself, *Joshua was a great leader of Israel, and God has a similar calling for me. Just as Joshua needed to learn about meditation, so do I. These words are spoken to me as much as to him. Now, in my own mind, how do I see them? How do I picture them? What does Joshua 1:8 look like on the canvas on my imagination?*

In the distance was a tree by the river with its roots slicing into the stream, going deep, finding watery spots that would never dry up. Perhaps David pondered verse and view, and in Psalm 1 he gave us his painting of Joshua 1.

Perfect Law

The New Testament writer James wasn't as expansive in his comments as David. He was plainspoken. His book reads more like the book of Proverbs than the book of Psalms. Yet James knew both Joshua 1 and Psalm 1, and he wanted to state the same truth in its simplest form. Thus we have James 1:25:

> Whoever looks intently into the perfect law that gives freedom, and continues in it—not forgetting what they have heard, but doing it—they will be blessed in what they do.

As we look intently into God's Word—just like Peter gazing into the empty tomb of Christ—as we see it, seek it, and submit to it, we will be blessed in what we do. We will be prosperous and successful. We will be like trees planted by rivers of water that yield fruitfulness in season.

Whenever you read a verse in the Bible, pause to think about it for a moment. Notice each word. Underline. Circle. Add an exclamation mark or a question mark. Read it emphasizing each word in turn. Examine it in a different translation. Jot it in your planner or pad. Take it into the day with you, and think about it throughout the day and into the night. Picture it as if you were picking up an artist's brush.

These three passages, which I discovered in a college dormitory more than forty years ago, became my reassurance in life. I didn't think I could be successful on my own, but I thought I could at least follow this simple formula. I could keep the Word of God on my mind by reading it daily, studying it regularly, and memorizing selected verses. I could train myself to meditate on it when I arose, as I walked through the day, as the evening descended, and when awakened during the night. With God's help, I could attempt to obey it. That was my part, and the rest— the success and prosperity and fruitfulness and blessings—were God's promises and represented His part of the equation.

I'll not presume to tell you I'm a successful person; I often feel a great sense of failure. But I know I'm more successful in the things that matter to God than I would be had I never found Joshua I, Psalm I, and James I.

You will be too.

God wants to impart heaven's success to your earthly life. He wants you to finish the work He's assigned you. He wants you to trust Him through the difficulties, rejoice amid the trials and along the trails of life, meet each day with a happy heart, and close every evening on a note of praise.

God wants to provide for your needs, guide your paths, bless your home, and use your witness. He promises to cause all things to work together for good for those who love Him, even when you

Quick Tip: Keep a Bible memory list—a set of note cards, pages in a journal, or an application on your phone. That way you can review them often and pound the verses into your brain like nails driven solidly into timber. Some verses are worth keeping near you for a lifetime.

can't imagine how. He wants to respond to your prayers with His unique answers. And when your work on earth is done, He wants to take you home to heaven, to a city with foundations whose builder and maker is God, to mansions prepared for you. And there, you will be able to worship Him for eternity, enjoy Him forever, be with those you love and who love you, and serve your Savior world without end.

> He promises to cause all things to work together for good for those who love Him, even when you can't imagine how.

I'd call that success, and that's worth meditating about.

For a free downloadable group study guide for this book as well as free personal audio meditation guides, visit www.robertjmorgan.com/meditation.

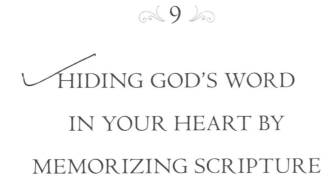

9

HIDING GOD'S WORD
IN YOUR HEART BY
MEMORIZING SCRIPTURE

I will also meditate on all Your work,
and talk of Your deeds.

—PSALM 77:12 NKJV

I've heard thousands of sermons in my life, but few equal the
one I heard by Rear Admiral Barry C. Black, Chaplain of
the United States Senate. His subject was "Something to Hold
On To."

Black, one of eight children, grew up in a dangerous Baltimore
neighborhood where drug pushers roamed the streets, prosti-
tutes loitered on the corners, and the staccato bark of gunfire

punctuated the weekends. One day Barry's mother came to Christ during an evangelistic meeting that included twelve subsequent weeks of biblical instruction. When she was afterward baptized, she was pregnant; and as she was immersed into the water, she asked the Lord to baptize her unborn child with the Holy Spirit.

That child was Barry, and he never knew a time when he didn't want to serve the Lord. As he wrote in *From the Hood to the Hill*, his mother was zealous about her children memorizing as much of the Bible as possible, and she offered a nickel a verse. Barry socked away vast numbers of verses. At first he specialized in the low-hanging fruit of very short verses, like John 11:35: "Jesus wept." But soon he began learning so many verses his mother changed the terms of the agreement to a flat quarter a week.

No amount of money, however, equaled the value of those verses in ensuing years. He told us how they saved him from a life of crime, from prison, and from throwing his life away. Throughout his life they had given him "something to hold on to."

As Chaplain Black preached to us, he tossed assorted Bible verses into his message as though plucking them from thin air. His mind was so stocked with Scripture that it permeated his presentation and his personality. In his closing remarks to us, he said it was the truth of the verses he had memorized and pondered throughout his life that gave him *Someone* to hold on to.[1]

Quick Tip: Read the Bible aloud to yourself. Your mind will pay better attention to words read orally and not just silently.

Proverbs 10:14 says, "The wise store up knowledge." Bible memorization is a great aid to meditation. It's not always absolutely essential, for we can jot down verses, keep them before our eyes, and remember the gist of them. Yet, when I stretch out in the hammock to close my eyes and meditate, I usually go to passages I've memorized.

- Deuteronomy 33:25
- Psalm 1
- Psalm 46
- Psalm 55:22 (and 1 Peter 5:7)
- Psalm 100
- Psalm 121
- Psalm 139:16
- Proverbs 3:5–6
- Isaiah 26:3–4
- Matthew 6:9–14
- John 14:1–6
- Romans 8:28
- Romans 15:13
- Philippians 4:4–9

And so on. Memory is a wonderful thing, and memorization is how we preserve our best memories. It might grow a bit harder to learn things by heart as we age, but instilling fresh material into our minds keeps us young.

As I read through the books of the Bible and study through its paragraphs, I always find some verses I want to memorize.

My son-in-law, Joshua Rowe, told me he meditates using a process of "slow memorization." He memorizes a single word or short phrase of a verse each day, but that portion becomes the scripture he takes into the day with him for meditation.

> Memory is a wonderful thing, and memorization is how we preserve our best memories.

Joshua also told me of his grandfather, Duane Mayhew, a World War II veteran, who took my book on Scripture memory, *100 Bible Verses Everyone Should Know by Heart,* and memorized all 100 verses before his death at age 93. These verses became his greatest source of meditation and comfort during his final days.

I have a simple technique that helps me immeasurably. It's the recorder on my phone. I have a feature on my smartphone that serves as a tape recorder, and it's an effective tool for Scripture memory.

Finding the passage I want to memorize (right now I'm working on James 1:19–25) I write it longhand in my little notebook. I repeat it over and over, a phrase at a time, day after day. Then I start quoting it into my recorder. Listening, I see what I've missed.

I've found that recording and listening to my memory verses several times each morning is a tremendous aid to memorizing the passage well enough to be able to quote it to myself and to others.

That passage from James 1 is particularly meaningful because, addressing itself to believers, verse 21 says: "Therefore, get rid of all moral filth and the evil that is so prevalent and humbly accept the word planted in you, which can save you."

As a believer I need to turn my thoughts from moral filth and the evil that is so prevalent. I need to humbly accept the implanted word—the word that is planted in my brain, the word I've received, learned, and perhaps memorized. I need to "look intently" into it and "continue" in it, not forgetting what I have heard, but doing it. Those who do so, promises James, "will be blessed in what they do" (James 1:25).

As I memorize, I don't try to rush. It may take me several weeks to inscribe a passage of Scripture onto the tablet of my memory, but speed isn't the object. I spent months on the six verses of Psalm 150. I'm not sure why that chapter was so difficult—I think it was its list of musical instruments—and I still go back and review it periodically. But I'm glad I learned it and, by reviewing it, I'll never forget it. There's not a better pick-me-up on earth than the words of Psalm 150, which begins, "Praise the LORD. Praise God in his sanctuary; praise him in his mighty heavens."

I wish I could singlehandedly revive the art of Scripture memorization in our homes and churches. There's no greater legacy to bequeath to our children than a storehouse of memory verses to draw upon their whole lives through.

Let's be like Ezra, who was "well versed" in Scripture (Ezra 7:6):

> There's no greater legacy to bequeath to our children than a storehouse of memory verses to draw upon their whole lives through.

The gracious hand of his God was on him. For Ezra had devoted himself to the study and observance of the Law of the LORD, and to teaching its decrees and laws in Israel. (Ezra 7:9–10)

Paul told Timothy:

From infancy you have known the Holy Scriptures, which are able to make you wise for salvation through faith in Christ Jesus. All Scripture is God-breathed and is useful for teaching, rebuking, correcting and training in righteousness, so that the servant of God may be thoroughly equipped for every good work. (2 Timothy 3:15–17)

The Bible—every word—is inspired, every promise is unfailing, every verse is a treasure. We're not to live by bread alone, but by every word proceeding from the mouth of God.

During the dark days of World War II, painter Paul Maze was alarmed by the terror sweeping across Europe. He escaped Bordeaux, fleeing from France to England, and he settled down uneasily in Hampshire. There, in his little room, he turned on his radio and listened to the intrepid speeches of Winston Churchill, whose words rallied the British Empire. Maze later wrote to Churchill, telling him, "Every word you said was like every drop of blood in a transfusion."[2]

And so it is for us with the Bible. Every word is like a transfusion of strength, of peace, of wisdom, of knowledge about both everyday life and eternal life.

For a free downloadable group study guide for this book as well as free personal audio meditation guides, visit www.robertjmorgan.com/meditation.

CONCLUSION:

Biblical Meditation Brings Intimacy with the Lord and Deep, Long-Lasting Joy

Draw near to God and He will draw near to you.

—James 4:8 nkjv

When I decided to work on a book about biblical meditation, I called my friend Dr. Roy King and asked him if he could think of a time when true, sustained biblical meditation had transformed his life and thoughts. He told me:

> The first thing that pops into my head was an experience I had as a student in the 1970s. I'd only been married a short period, and I began struggling with depression. This was new to me, because I'd never been depressed before and I didn't know what was happening. I endured

a battery of physical tests, but nothing seemed wrong. Yet I was in a very dark place, and I struggled to get up and go out every day. I was especially afraid my marriage would fail. I'd grown up in a dysfunctional home with an alcoholic mother who had mental issues. I'd never talked about these things, but they were now haunting me.

I finally reached out to my best friend, Ron Barker, who lived in Texas. I called him and told him I was really struggling. Ron listened for quite a while; then he said, "Okay. Now, I've got one thing I want you to do. I want you to study Ephesians 1:3–14 every day. Don't read anything else in the Bible during your devotional time. Stay in that passage. Read it in different translations. Outline it. Study each word. Analyze it as if you were back in your high school grammar class. Think about it. Ponder it. Stay in Ephesians 1 until God makes it real in your heart."

Roy continued:

I didn't have anything to lose, so I started doing that, mechanically at first. I really had no desire to do it, but I stayed with it. I copied it on cards, carried it around, and read it every day.

My wife, Pandora, and I had a little baby and moved

to Asheville, North Carolina. One night I couldn't sleep, and I got up—it was one or two o'clock in the morning—and I sat in the living room of our small apartment. I turned on the lamp by the rocking chair, picked up my Bible, and turned to Ephesians I.

Suddenly that passage came alive as if on fire. It was the illuminating work of the Holy Spirit. It just suddenly came alive, and I began to see what it really meant to me, to my personality, what it meant to be in Christ and to inherit all the truths in those verses—the forgiveness, redemption, adoption, the sealing of the Holy Spirit, the riches of His grace. None of it depended on my being a perfect child or trying to heal my parents' marriage. None of it was hindered by my background or baggage. I started journaling as fast as I could and I wrote until dawn.

I had been walking around talking about myself as being worthless, a failure. But that night, it was almost like a voice saying audibly, "You should never call yourself worthless again. Look at how valuable you are to Me and how much I've done for you and given to you." That night was a turning point in my life. That night I learned the power of biblical meditation.[1]

I'm asking God to use this little book to help you reclaim the art and learn the power of biblical meditation. Let God change the way you think. His thoughts are not your thoughts, but they should be and they can be—increasingly, victoriously—through a commitment to develop the mind of Christ.

Ours is a shallow age. Our thoughts are shallow, superficial, and empty. But God wants people who will live hallowed lives in a hollow world. Biblical meditation is a key way to build depth and substance into who we are and who we're coming to be. We are transformed by the renewing of our minds.

> God wants people who will live hallowed lives in a hollow world.

Commit to His lordship and study His Word daily, like the noble Bereans in Acts 17:11. Let your mind mull over Scripture as you arise; ponder it when you retire; think about it as you go about your day and as you slumber at night. Use biblical meditation to build yourself up and calm yourself down. Teach your children to meditate. Share the truths of this book with others and consider using it in group studies. Begin standing in God's council and walking in His presence.

Let me end with these words from the Lord in Proverbs 7:1–3:

Live according to what I am telling you;
    guard my instructions as you would a treasure *deep*
        within you.
Stay true to my directives, and they will serve you well;
    make my teachings the lens through which you see life.
Bind cords around your fingers *to remind you of them;*
    meditate on them, and you'll engrave them upon your heart.
        (THE VOICE)

10-DAY MEDITATION GUIDE

*H*ow to use this guide:

Based on the contents of each chapter and the conclusion of *Reclaiming the Lost Art of Biblical Meditation*, I've selected ten scriptures for further contemplation. Each day, find a quiet place without interruption and work through the passages on the following pages, using a plan based on our definition of biblical meditation: pondering, personalizing, and practicing God's Word.

- Ponder: Read the passage at the top of each page attentively, perhaps aloud. If you have time, read the passage in the fuller context I suggest. Imagine the Lord speaking these words to you in a personal way. Take time to focus your attention on each word and seek to understand what the passage means.

- Personalize: Now consider what this passage means to you. Read it meditatively using the bullet points I've provided to prompt your thoughts. Don't think of this as an academic exercise but as personal reflection. Let God speak to your heart as you mull over the verses He's given you in Scripture. If the Lord were sitting down beside you and speaking these words audibly to you, what verse, phrase, word, truth, command, or promise would affect you most deeply?

- Practice: At the end of your time, jot down that verse or phrase to take with you into the day. You might write it on a note card, a page in your calendar, or an easily retrievable place on your phone. Review it all day, as you shower, drive, walk, work, or rest. Think about it as you fall asleep tonight. Try sharing it with someone. Put into practice and do whatever it says.

Ten passages, ten minutes, ten days . . . and you'll soon be meditating on scriptures from Genesis to Revelation, day and night. The secret is letting Bible verses circulate through your mind like water through a fountain. As you listen to the voice of Jesus through meditation on His Word, you'll find true peace in Him.

Let *the words from* the book of the law be always on your lips. Meditate on them day and night so that you may be careful to live by all that is written in it. If you do, as

you make your way *through this world*, you will prosper and
always find success.

JOSHUA 1:8 (THE VOICE)

Meditation Guide for Chapter 1

Romans 12:1–2
[For a fuller meditation, read Romans 12:1–8]

1. Ponder

   *Therefore, I urge you, brothers and sisters, in view of God's mercy,
   to offer your bodies as a living sacrifice, holy and pleasing to God—this
   is your true and proper worship. Do not conform to the pattern of this
   world, but be transformed by the renewing of your mind. Then you will
   test and approve what God's will is—his good, pleasing and perfect will.*

2. Personalize

   *Therefore, I urge you, brothers and sisters, in view of God's mercy,
   to offer your bodies as a living sacrifice, holy and pleasing to God—this is
   your true and proper worship.*

   Contemplate the word "urge." Can you think of a time
   when someone "urged" you to do (or not to do) something?
   How did you feel? What is this verse urging you to do?

Think of your body. In what way can it become a "living sacrifice"? What does that mean to you?

Do not conform to the pattern of this world . . .

Can you think of ways in which you are conforming to the pattern of this world? If you were a ship, would any water be seeping through the hull, or is your life morally and spiritually waterproof? Is any worldliness trickling into your habits?

. . . but be transformed by the renewing of your mind.

Mull over the three significant words of this verse: *transformed, renewing, mind.* Visualize your brain. What would happen were God to "transform" it?

Then you will be able to test and approve what God's will is—his good, pleasing, and perfect will.

This indicates God has a plan for your life. What are the conditions for discovering it? Do these two verses aptly describe your life?

3. Practice

Write down a verse or phrase from this passage to take with you into the day and quote to yourself. For me, it was, "Offer your bodies a living sacrifice." That's a command, and it's visual. In the Old Testaments, the sacrifices were slain, but I'm to offer my body as a "living sacrifice." That phrase is worth thinking about all day long.

Meditation Guide for Chapter 2

James 3:17
[For a fuller meditation, read James 3:13–17]

1. Ponder

*But the wisdom that comes down from heaven is first of all pure;
then peace-loving; considerate, submissive, full of mercy and good fruit,
impartial and sincere.*

2. Personalize

But the wisdom that comes down from heaven . . .

Find a way of visualizing wisdom—perhaps a book or a
bright cloud or an entire library or a dove or a bolt of lightning. See it coming down from heaven, descending, ready to
connect with your mind. If you were struck with the lightning
bolt of God's wisdom from above, how would it light up your
life? The following words suggest an answer.

Is first of all pure . . .

Are there areas of impurity in your life? How would the
wisdom from above deal with those areas?

. . . then peace-loving . . .

Have you had any conflicts recently? How would you
have handled them differently had you approached them
with the wisdom of God?

. . . considerate . . .

Review how you've treated people today. Would they use this word to describe you?

. . . submissive . . .

When did you last exhibit a submissive attitude in a situation?

. . . full of mercy and good fruit, impartial and sincere.

Which of those terms best describes you? Which least describes you?

3. Practice

What part of this passage seems the most meaningful to you today? Jot it down and keep thinking about it through the day and night. How can you translate it into a different set of attitudes or actions?

_____

_____

_____

_____

_____

_____

_____

Meditation Guide for Chapter 3

2 Peter I:3–4
[For a fuller meditation, read 2 Peter I:I–II]

1. Ponder

His divine power has given us everything we need for a godly life through our knowledge of him who called us by his own glory and goodness. Through these he has given us his very great and precious promises so that through them you may participate in the divine nature, having escaped the corruption in the world caused by evil desires.

2. Personalize

His divine power has given us everything we need . . . .

Each word in this phrase is powerful. Read it repeatedly, emphasizing each word, letting the emphasis soak into your mind.

. . . for a godly life . . .

Why has God's divine power given us all we need? What is His desired outcome? What does the word "godly" really mean? Does that word describe you?

. . . through our knowledge of him who called us by his own glory and goodness.

What attributes of God caused Him to call us and give us everything we need?

Through these he has given us his very great and precious promises so that through them you may participate in the divine nature, having escaped the corruption in the world caused by evil desires.

How are God's promises to you described? Can you think of some biblical promises that are very great and precious to you? Why has God given these promises to you? In what way can we "participate in the divine nature"?

3. Practice

This passage has some tremendous phrases—*His divine power . . . everything we need . . . His own glory and goodness . . . very great and precious promises . . . participate in the divine nature . . . having escaped the corruption in the world . . .* Find a phrase in these verses to ponder all day today, and go to sleep thinking about its significance. How could your mind-set be changed because of these verses?

_____

_____

_____

_____

_____

_____

Meditation Guide for Chapter 4

Luke 2:17–19
[For a fuller meditation, read Luke 2:1–20]

1. Ponder

When they had seen him, they spread the word concerning what had been told them about this child, and all who heard it were amazed at what the shepherds said to them. But Mary treasured up all these things and pondered them in her heart.

2. Personalize

When they had seen him . . .

This is referring to the shepherds who hurried to Bethlehem to see the Christ child. Many people only read this passage at Christmas, but spend some time visualizing it now—that wondrous night, the shepherds' fields, the angelic host, the holy family in a stable, the Baby in the manger.

. . . they spread the word concerning what had been told them about this child . . .

These shepherds couldn't help but tell everyone what they had seen and heard. Imagine their excitement. Put yourself in their sandals. When was the last time you were as excited to "spread the word"?

. . . and all who heard it were amazed at what the shepherds said to them.

Focus on that word "amazed." Try to visualize the faces and reactions of the people. What most amazes you today about the Lord Jesus Christ?

But Mary treasured up all these things and pondered them in her heart.

Use your imagination to paint a mental picture of Mary. What does it mean to treasure something? How do we ponder things? In what way is this a description of the process of meditation? What truths are you treasuring up and pondering today from God's Word?

3. Practice

Think about the things you treasure most. As you go into the rest of the day, use that word "treasure" to cultivate a sense of the richness you have in the blessings that came down from heaven with the baby Jesus. Thank God for these treasures, one by one. Let this be a day of amazement and thanksgiving. Live in the enthusiasm of Jesus all day.

_____

_____

_____

_____

_____

_____

Meditation Guide for Chapter 5

Jeremiah 15:16–16

[For a fuller meditation, read Jeremiah 15:10–21]

I. Ponder

LORD, you understand; remember me and care for me. Avenge me on my persecutors. You are long-suffering—do not take me away; think of how I suffer reproach for your sake. When your words came, I ate them; they were my joy and my heart's delight, for I bear your name, LORD God Almighty.

2. Personalize

LORD, you understand . . .

Let those three words soak into your soul. Think of your current struggles. Turn these three words into a personal prayer. What does God understand about your circumstances? Does He understand the situation better than you do?

. . . remember me and care for me.

Since the Lord understands, you can ask Him to remember you and to care for you: "Care for me!"

Avenge me on my persecutors. You are long-suffering—do not take me away; think of how I suffer reproach for your sake.

Are you being persecuted? Is someone putting pressure on you because of your allegiance to Christ? Or is someone causing you anxiety in some way?

When your words came, I ate them . . .

What does it mean to eat God's words? Can you think of other times when the Bible compares the study of Scripture to eating? How is the physical activity of eating food like the spiritual activity of studying and digesting Scripture? If you had to write a menu of your recent mental diet—whether it was junk food or enriching—what would it be?

. . . they were my joy and my heart's delight, for I bear your name, Lord God Almighty.

Think of some verses that have recently been your joy and heart's delight.

3. Practice

Jeremiah knew the power of meditation, and he compared it to eating and digesting God's Word. It gave him strength and sustenance to withstand the pressures of his day. Find a phrase or verse here and chew on it as you go through the day. Learn to devour and digest Bible verses like a hungry person devouring and digesting a five-course meal.

_____

_____

_____

_____

_____

Meditation Guide for Chapter 6

Philippians 4:8
[For a fuller meditation, read Philippians 4:3–9]

I. Ponder

Finally, brothers and sisters, whatever is true, whatever is noble, whatever is right, whatever is pure, whatever is lovely, whatever is admirable—if anything is excellent or praiseworthy—think about such things.

2. Personalize

Finally brothers and sisters, . . .

When a speaker or writer uses the word "finally," what does it say about the subject he's about to bring up?

. . . whatever is true . . .

Go to the end of the verse and notice that the writer, the apostle Paul, is giving us a set of criteria for the things we should think about. We should think about things that are true. If your mind dwells on things that are true, what will you be thinking about?

. . . whatever is noble, . . .

What does this word bring to mind? What does it mean to be noble? If we're thinking about things that are noble, what would they be?

. . . whatever is right, . . .

Some things are right to think about and some are wrong to think about. Are you harboring any wrong thoughts? How can you replace them with right thoughts?

. . . whatever is pure, whatever is lovely, whatever is admirable—if anything is excellent or praiseworthy—think about such things.

Keep taking these words one at a time. Could someone use those words to describe you? Your thoughts?

3. Practice

The verse gets to the heart of biblical meditation. The words Paul chose are a perfect description of our Lord and of His Word. Take this verse into the day with you, considering it the criteria that should determine what you think about today.

_____

_____

_____

_____

_____

_____

_____

_____

_____

Meditation Guide for Chapter 7

Psalm 143:8

[For a fuller meditation, read Psalm 143]

1. Ponder

Let the morning bring me word of your unfailing love, for I have put my trust in you. Show me the way I should go, for to you I entrust my life.

2. Personalize

Let the morning . . .

Why does the Psalmist want word of God's unfailing love in the morning? What's special about the morning?

. . . bring me word of your unfailing love, . . .

The writer doesn't say, "Bring me a feeling . . ." or "Give me an impression." What's the significance of the word, "word"? What's the meaning of "unfailing"? How many people or circumstances can be described that way? Can you think of other verses in the Bible that describe God's love for you?

. . . for I have put my trust in you.

Notice the word "for." That indicates our trust in the Lord paves the way for the Lord to give us word of His unfailing love. Try putting this verse in your own words, which is a great meditation technique. For example, you might say, "Since I am trusting you, make sure I don't miss the morning reminders of your daily love that will never let me down."

Show me the way I should go, for to you I entrust my life.

Make this a specific prayer: "Show me the way I should go in the decisions before me, in this dilemma, in this problem, with this situation . . ." The Psalmist bases his prayer on the fact he entrusts his life to the Lord. Think through this sentence. If we entrust our very lives to the Lord, we can trust Him to help us with our daily decisions, especially when we recall His unfailing love every morning.

3. Practice

This is a short verse, and you can probably memorize it faster than you think. What a great verse to offer as a prayer upon awakening. Whether memorized or not, try quoting it to yourself aloud every morning for the next few days. Let its encouragement brighten your day.

Meditation Guide for Chapter 8

Joshua 1:8–9

[For a fuller meditation, read Joshua 1:1–9]

1. Ponder

Keep this Book of the Law always on your lips; meditate on it day and night, so that you may be careful to do everything written in it. Then you will be prosperous and successful. Have I not commanded you? Be strong and courageous. Do not be afraid; do not be discouraged, for the Lord *your God will be with you wherever you go.*

2. Personalize

Keep this Book of the Law always on your lips . . .

Is the Word of God always on your lips? What does that mean and how can you fulfill this command more fully?

. . . meditate on it day and night, so that you may be careful to do everything written in it.

This is a key passage about meditation. On the basis of this verse, ask yourself: "On what should I be meditating? How often should I meditate? What should be the result of my personal practice of meditation?"

Then you will be prosperous and successful.

What do these words, "prosperous" and "successful," mean from God's point of view? If, from his perspective, I'm prosperous and successful, what will I be like or look like?

Have I not commanded you? Be strong and courageous. Do not be afraid; do not be discouraged, for the LORD your God will be with you wherever you go.

Focus on each of these short phrases as though the Lord were sitting beside you, speaking each word to you slowly and with emphasis. Which phrase do you most need today? Don't overlook the word "commanded." That indicates these are not suggestions. These are the attitudes God commands us to display in our lives.

3. Practice

The first paragraph of the book of Joshua is full of encouragement. Moses had died, and these were God's words of encouragement to Joshua as he assumed leadership of the Israelites and prepared to lead them into the promised land. Verses 8 and 9 are especially rich. What phrase from this passage do you need to remember all day long?

_____

_____

_____

_____

_____

_____

Meditation Guide for Chapter 9

2 Timothy 3:16–17

[For a fuller meditation, read 2 Timothy 3:10–4:5]

1. Ponder

All Scripture is God-breathed and is useful for teaching, rebuking, correcting and training in righteousness, so that the servant of God may be thoroughly equipped for every good work.

2. Personalize

All Scripture . . .

Mentally review every book of the Bible you can think of and every familiar text. Think of books in the Bible you've never read or seldom read. What's the significance of that word "all"?

. . . is God-breathed . . .

Contemplate the meaning of this. Think about the relationship of breathing and speaking. Is it possible to speak without exhaling air? Marvel at the creative genius of God, who created our lungs, tongues, vocal cords, and speech patterns. Now visualize God breathing out his Word.

. . . and is useful for teaching, rebuking, correcting and training in righteousness . . .

Think about the relationship of the four impacts of

Scripture listed here. Why are they listed in this order? How does one lead to another?

. . . so that the servant of God may be thoroughly equipped for every good work.

Why has God given us his inspired word? If every word is God-breathed, does that mean every word can lead to this result? Think of the adverb "thoroughly." Think of the word "equipped." What does it mean to be equipped? Why does God want us to be thoroughly equipped, and what happens if we aren't?

3. Practice

This is one of the Bible's key passages on the inspiration and authority of Scripture. Notice the all-inclusive words: *All . . . thoroughly . . . every.* If you'll become very familiar with this verse and its context, your appreciation for the memorization and meditation of Scripture will grow. If this verse is true—as it is—it should make a difference in the way we interact with Scripture. How can you go to the next level in recovering the lost art of biblical meditation?

_____

_____

_____

_____

_____

_____

_____

_____

_____

_____

_____

_____

_____

_____

_____

_____

_____

_____

_____

_____

_____

_____

_____

_____

_____

_____

_____

_____

Meditation Guide for the Conclusion

Ephesians 1:3

[For a fuller meditation, read Ephesians 1:1–14]

1. Ponder

   Praise be to the God and Father of our Lord Jesus Christ, who has blessed us in the heavenly realms with every spiritual blessing in Christ.

2. Personalize

   Praise . . .

   It's easy to determine the opening theme of the book of Ephesians. The writer, Paul, opens the body of his letter with this word: "Praise." Before going on with the verse and learning what Paul was praising God for, spend some time praising Him yourself. Think of His qualities, His vastness, His goodness. Think of His blessings, of answered prayers. Think of hymns or songs that are praise-oriented.

   . . . be to the God and Father of our Lord Jesus Christ . . .

   This verse refers to God the Father and God the Son. Later in chapter 1, Paul will rejoice in God the Holy Spirit (verse 13). Contemplating the Trinity is mind-boggling, but also mind-expanding. Think of the mystery of one God who eternally dwells in three persons—Father, Son, and Holy Spirit. What does each of the persons of the Godhead mean to you?

. . . who has blessed us . . .

Think of who the "us" is in your life. How has God blessed you and yours? Now, quote this verse aloud and replace "us" with "me." Make it personal. Make it your prayer: "Praise be to the God and Father of my Lord Jesus Christ who has blessed me!" How has he blessed you? Count your blessings. Try to think of things for which you have never before thanked God. Are there blessings you've never turned into items of thanksgiving?

. . . in the heavenly realms with every spiritual blessing in Christ.

Try to visualize this. If you have time, read through the first chapters of Ephesians to see how Paul used the phrases "heavenly realms" and "in Christ."

3. Practice

Catch the exuberance of this verse and let its enthusiasm set the thermostat of your emotions today. How would your personality and mind-set be heightened today if you kept this verse at the forefront of your thinking every moment of this day?

_____

_____

_____

_____

SCRIPTURES TO MEDITATE ON

Deuteronomy 7:9

Know therefore that the LORD your God is God; he is the faithful God, keeping his covenant of love to a thousand generations of those who love him and keep his commandments.

Joshua 1:9

"Have I not commanded you? Be strong and courageous. Do not be afraid; do not be discouraged, for the LORD your God will be with you wherever you go."

2 Samuel 22:2–3

The LORD is my rock, my fortress and my deliverer;
my God is my rock, in whom I take refuge,
my shield and the horn of my salvation.
He is my stronghold, my refuge and my savior—
from violent people you save me.

Psalm 18:2

The LORD is my rock, my fortress and my deliverer;
    my God is my rock, in whom I take refuge,
    my shield and the horn of my salvation, my stronghold.

Psalm 25:4–5

Show me your ways, LORD,
    teach me your paths.
Guide me in your truth and teach me,
    for you are God my Savior,
    and my hope is in you all day long.

Psalm 27:1

The LORD is my light and my salvation—
    whom shall I fear?
The LORD is the stronghold of my life—
    of whom shall I be afraid?

Psalm 51:10–12

Create in me a pure heart, O God,
    and renew a steadfast spirit within me.

Do not cast me from your presence
  or take your Holy Spirit from me.
Restore to me the joy of your salvation
  and grant me a willing spirit, to sustain me.

Proverbs 3:3–4

Let love and faithfulness never leave you;
  bind them around your neck,
    write them on the tablet of your heart.
Then you will win favor and a good name
  in the sight of God and man.

Proverbs 3:5–6

Trust in the LORD with all your heart
  and lean not on your own understanding;
in all your ways submit to him,
  and he will make your paths straight.

Isaiah 12:2

Surely God is my salvation;
  I will trust and not be afraid.
The LORD, the LORD himself, is my strength and my defense;
  he has become my salvation.

Isaiah 41:10

"So do not fear, for I am with you;
    do not be dismayed, for I am your God.
I will strengthen you and help you;
    I will uphold you with my righteous right hand."

Jeremiah 6:16

"Stand at the crossroads and look;
    ask for the ancient paths,
ask where the good way is, and walk in it,
    and you will find rest for your souls."

Zephaniah 3:17

"The Lord your God is with you,
    the Mighty Warrior who saves.
He will take great delight in you;
    in his love he will no longer rebuke you,
    but will rejoice over you with singing."

Matthew 6:19–21

"Do not store up for yourselves treasures on earth, where moths and vermin destroy, and where thieves break in and steal. But store up for yourselves treasures in heaven, where moths and vermin do not destroy, and where thieves do not break in and steal. For where your treasure is, there your heart will be also."

Matthew 6:31–34

"So do not worry, saying, 'What shall we eat?' or 'What shall we drink?' or 'What shall we wear?' For the pagans run after all these things, and your heavenly Father knows that you need them. But seek first his kingdom and his righteousness, and all these things will be given to you as well. Therefore do not worry about tomorrow, for tomorrow will worry about itself. Each day has enough trouble of its own."

Matthew 28:18–20

Then Jesus came to them and said, "All authority in heaven and on earth has been given to me. Therefore go and make disciples of all nations, baptizing them in the name of the Father and of the Son and of the Holy Spirit, and teaching them to obey everything I have commanded you. And surely I am with you always, to the very end of the age."

John 14:27

"Peace I leave with you; my peace I give you. I do not give to you as the world gives. Do not let your hearts be troubled and do not be afraid."

Romans 12:1–2

Therefore, I urge you, brothers and sisters, in view of God's mercy, to offer your bodies as a living sacrifice, holy and pleasing to God—this is your true and proper worship. Do not conform to the pattern of this world, but be transformed by the renewing of your mind. Then you will be able to test and approve what God's will is—his good, pleasing and perfect will.

1 Corinthians 10:13

No temptation has overtaken you except what is common to mankind. And God is faithful; he will not let you be tempted beyond what you can bear. But when you are tempted, he will also provide a way out so that you can endure it.

2 Corinthians 12:9

But he said to me, "My grace is sufficient for you, for my power is made perfect in weakness." Therefore I will boast all the more gladly about my weaknesses, so that Christ's power may rest on me.

Galatians 2:20

I have been crucified with Christ and I no longer live, but Christ lives in me. The life I now live in the body, I live by faith in the Son of God, who loved me and gave himself for me.

Ephesians 2:8–10

For it is by grace you have been saved, through faith—and this is not from yourselves, it is the gift of God—not by works, so that no one can boast. For we are God's handiwork, created in Christ Jesus to do good works, which God prepared in advance for us to do.

Philippians 4:6–7

Do not be anxious about anything, but in every situation, by prayer and petition, with thanksgiving, present your requests to God. And the peace of God, which transcends all understanding, will guard your hearts and your minds in Christ Jesus.

Philippians 4:8

Finally, brothers and sisters, whatever is true, whatever is noble, whatever is right, whatever is pure, whatever is lovely, whatever is admirable—if anything is excellent or praiseworthy—think about such things.

Colossians 3:12–13

Therefore, as God's chosen people, holy and dearly loved, clothe yourselves with compassion, kindness, humility, gentleness and patience. Bear with each other and forgive one another if any of you has a grievance against someone. Forgive as the Lord forgave you.

Hebrews 4:12

For the word of God is alive and active. Sharper than any double-edged sword, it penetrates even to dividing soul and spirit, joints and marrow; it judges the thoughts and attitudes of the heart.

James 1:2–4

Consider it pure joy, my brothers and sisters, whenever you face trials of many kinds, because you know that the testing of your faith produces perseverance. Let perseverance finish its work so that you may be mature and complete, not lacking anything.

1 John 3:16–18

This is how we know what love is: Jesus Christ laid down his life for us. And we ought to lay down our lives for our brothers and sisters. If anyone has material possessions and sees a brother or sister in need but has no pity on them, how can the love of God be in that person? Dear children, let us not love with words or speech but with actions and in truth.

ACKNOWLEDGMENTS

I want to thank my friends at HarperCollins—Laura Minchew, Kristen Parrish, Michael Aulisio, and their teams—along with my agents, Sealy and Matt Yates. I'm also grateful to my associates at Clearly Media for their great work with my websites and social media ministries. I also owe a debt of gratitude to my assistant, Sherry Anderson, and to Casey Pontious for her help with this project.

My wife, Katrina, as usual, read repeated drafts of this book, and her comments led to a better manuscript.

NOTES

Epigraph

1. J. I. Packer, *Knowing God* (Downers Grove, IL: InterVarsity Press, 1973), 18–19.

Introduction

1. From the headings and text of the *New International Version*.
2. Some of these general insights came from attending a Basic Youth Conflicts Institute in 1973, and I'm indebted for the concept of "memorizing, visualizing, and personalizing" verses of Scripture and the concept of wisdom as "seeing life from God's point of view."

Chapter 1: Why Is Biblical Meditation Important?

1. Sarah Bradford, *Harriet Tubman: The Moses of Her People* (New York: Geo. R. Lockwood & Son, 1897), 24–25. The quotation has been edited to remove colloquialisms.
2. Kate B. Wilkinson, "May the Mind of Christ, My Savior," published sometime before 1913.

Chapter 2: Biblical Meditation: Focusing on the Wonder of God and Gaining Perspective

1. Jennifer Rothschild, *Lessons I Learned in the Dark: Steps to Walking by Faith, Not by Sight* (Colorado Springs: Multnomah Books, 2002), 51.
2. Solomon Ginsburg, *A Wandering Jew in Brazil* (Nashville: Sunday School Board, Southern Baptist Convention, 1922), 169–170.

3. Charles Spurgeon, "Christ's Indwelling Word," a sermon preached at the Metropolitan Tabernacle, Newington, on Sunday night, April 10, 1881.

4. Thulia Susannah Henderson, *Daily Bible Teachings* (London: Knight and Son, 1859), 32.

Chapter 3: Biblical Meditation: Seeing Yourself as the Lord Sees You

1. https://nccih.nih.gov/research/statistics/NHIS/2012/mind-body/meditation.

2. David McCullough, *Truman* (New York: Simon & Schuster, 1992), 623.

3. Fanny Crosby, "Redeemed, How I Love to Proclaim It," published in *Songs of Redeeming Love* (Philadelphia: 1882).

4. Samuel Clarke, *A Collection of the Sweet Assuring Promises of Scripture* (New York: Lane & Scott, 1848), 10–11.

5. Rosalind Goforth, *How I Know God Answers Prayer* (New York: Harper & Brother Publishers, 1921), 51–52, http://www.gutenberg.org/files/26033/26033-h/26033-h.htm.

6. Barbara Hudson Powers, *The Henrietta Mears Story* (Old Tappan, NJ: Fleming H. Revell, 1957), 61–62, http://ccel.us/mears.toc.html.

Chapter 4: Biblical Meditation: Calming Your Spirit and Finding Peace

1. Based on a personal conversation and exchange of email, and used with permission.

2. Charles Stanley, *How to Listen to God* (Nashville: Thomas Nelson, 1985), 109.

3. Billy Graham, *Just As I Am* (Nashville: HarperCollins Christian, 1997), 7.

4. Maurice Pink, in a personal interview with the author, January 1, 2012. Used with permission.

5. I tell this story in my book *The Lord Is My Shepherd* (Nashville: Howard Books, 2013), xvii–xix.

6. Elmer Towns, *Praying the Lord's Prayer for Spiritual Breakthrough* (Minneapolis: Bethany House, 1997), 30–31, Kindle location 395–405.

7. Bob Pittman, *Chosen: The Mission and Message of Frank Pollard* (Jackson, MS: Franklin Printers, Inc., 2002), 72.

Chapter 5: Biblical Meditation: Helping You Understand God's Word

1. See, for example, Sean Macaulay, "Anthony Hopkins Interview," *Telegraph*, January 31, 2011, at www.telegraph.co.uk/culture/film /starsandstories/8286801/Anthony-Hopkins-interview.html.

2. Matt Gardner, in a personal conversation with the author. Used with permission.

3. David Saxton, *God's Battle Plan for the Mind* (Grand Rapids: Reformation Heritage Books, 2015), 61.

4. Sam Doherty, *A Life Worth Living* (Lisburn, Northern Ireland: Child Evangelism Fellowship, 2010), 213–214.

5. Ruth Bell Graham, *It's My Turn* (Old Tappan, NJ: Fleming H. Revell, 1982), 37.

6. *A Primer on Meditation* (Colorado Springs: The Navigators, n.d.), 3.

7. James M. Gray, *How to Master the English Bible* (Edinburgh and London: Oliphant Anderson & Ferrier, 1907), 53.

8. Ed Reese, *The Life and Ministry of Jonathan Edwards* (Glenwood, IL: Fundamental Publishers, 1975), 12.

9. Attributed to Bernard Barton, 1826.

Chapter 6: Biblical Meditation: Gaining Insight into God's Will

1. Robert J. Morgan, *The Red Sea Rules* (Nashville: W Publishing, 2014), xi–xii.

Chapter 7: Techniques for Effective Meditation

1. Samuel Logan Brengle, *The Soul Winner's Secret* (London: Salvation Army Publishing Department, 1903), 29.

2. I previously told this story in my book *Every Child, Every Nation, Every Day* (Warrenton, MO: CEF Press, 2015), 59–60.

3. André Castelot, *Napoleon: A Biography by André Castelot* (New York: Ishi Press, 2009), from notes in my files.

4. Rosalind Goforth, *Climbing* (Wheaton, IL: Sword Book Club, 1946), 16–17.

5. Stephen King, *On Writing* (New York: Scribner, 2000), 203.

6. Clarence W. Hall, *Samuel Logan Brengle* (Atlanta: Salvation Army Supplies and Purchasing Department, 1933), 182–184.

7. Leslie B. Flynn, *Your Inner You* (Wheaton, IL: Victor Books, 1984), 47.

Chapter 8: Finding Godly Success God's Way

1. J. I. Packer, *Knowing God* (Downers Grove, IL: InterVarsity Press, 1973), 18–19.

2. David Saxton, *God's Battle Plan for the Mind* (Grand Rapids: Reformation Heritage Books, 2015), 7.

3. This story is related, among other places, in D.C. Gonzalez, *The Art of Mental Training* (GonzoLane Media, 2013), 28–29, and Gary Mack and David Casstevens, *Mind Gym* (McGraw-Hill, 2002), 15–16.

Chapter 9: Hiding God's Word in Your Heart by Memorizing Scripture

1. Chaplain Barry Black, "Something to Hold On To," a sermon delivered at the Mandarin Oriental Hotel in Washington, DC, April 9, 2016, from my notes.

2. William Manchester and Paul Reid, *The Last Lion: Winston Spencer Churchill: Defender of the Realm, 1940–1965* (New York: Bantam Books, 2013), 185.

Conclusion

1. Dr. Roy King, in conversations and correspondence with the author. Used with permission.